A Full Life in Sitka, Alaska

Martin R. Strand, Sr.

iUniverse, Inc.
New York   Bloomington

A Full Life in Sitka, Alaska

iUniverse books may be ordered through booksellers or by contacting:

iUniverse
1663 Liberty Drive
Bloomington, IN 47403
www.iuniverse.com
1-800-Authors (1-800-288-4677)

Because of the dynamic nature of the Internet, any Web addresses or links contained in this book may have changed since publication and may no longer be valid.

ISBN: 978-1-4502-5051-1 (sc)
ISBN: 978-1-4502-5052-8 (ebk)

Printed in the United States of America

iUniverse rev. date: 10/22/2010

Martin Strand

DEDICATION

This book is written by Martin R. Strand,

a Kaagwaantaan man named K'wách'

In memory of our ancestors and Tlingit elders

Kiksádi & Kaagwaantaan

and is lovingly dedicated to our grandchildren: Lila

Denali

Gary

Ben

Tyler

Shelby

FORWARD

Pat Sheahan

My friend Monty Wilson went to school with Martin and would almost always comment after an encounter with him, that, "he has always marched to the beat of a different drum." Martin Strand came off at first impression as peculiar. Known as Brother Martin he had a way of presenting himself at first with comedic one liners that disarmed and made new acquaintances feel comfortable. But it also made an impression that he had a silly disposition. In fact, Martin was observing and reflecting and appreciated everything and everyone around him with an astute sense, guided by the conviction that all were important, even sacred.

First impressions are often deceiving. Martin belonged to many groups and to many people. He didn't always enjoy being front and center, however. Rather, he participated in his complicated social world with the ironic eye of an outsider looking in, simultaneously showing solidarity and yet sometimes feeling himself partly outside and on the margins. It is that rare combination, albeit contradictory, that gave him that blessed gift of poetry and artistry.

As to his work, Brother Martin is significant because his words and the images he captured represent an important but confusing time for some Sitkans, especially those that are residents year round over the course of decades. I will try to explain. Martin was "old school". He belonged to the Alaska Native Brotherhood (ANB) because his grandfather's heart "bled ANB".

This group is itself an interesting combination of people, holding to tradition and embracing modern realities. Martin was a man in two worlds

On the one hand, he was never as animated as when we went hunting and fishing in the traditional grounds around Sitka Sound. There he hunted seal and recalled trips with his family to fish camp when he was young. He took pride in his status at Dog Point Fish camp, where he had a bedroom dedicated to him for when he would come to teach any student who was interested in catching and preparing salmon. Martin taught me about marksmanship and ethics and friendship. We reloaded ammunition together and told stories and dreamed about future excursions.

What we caught, we shared. And we went to ANB meetings together. It was there that I witnessed his allegiance to his clan and to the memory of those Native peoples that had gone on before him. Martin's identity is tied to the Kaagwaantaan clan and nothing made him more proud than that affiliation.

But Martin was a Renaissance man, too. He grew up in the cottages of Sheldon Jackson College, somewhat separate from the traditional native neighborhoods of Sitka. He may have been only a mile away, but Martin would pay a price of this separation by being on the fringes socially. The reward, however, was the chance to be mobile and to expand his opportunities.

He motorcycled across Canada and the U.S. He went to the University in Ohio. He learned piano, hustled people in pool halls, took up photography. At home, Martin ventured into radio broadcasting and computers. He enjoyed bicycles and socialized in any place that might be susceptible to a story in exchange for a cup of coffee or tea. He took up the art of peacemaking and mediation.

And he watched things carefully, documenting people, times and events with an eye toward tribute, not judgment. He was as apt to quote a French philosopher as he was a Native Elder. Watching Martin watch others, I have often wondered how those seas of influence converged in his mind. I believe he used his crafts as a way of maintaining sanity and letting things stand on their own merit. And we are the recipients of his creative compartmentalizing. Creative endeavor is by nature both limiting and expressive.

Martin Strand will also be remembered for being friendly. When I had coffee with him, I was amazed at how many people he knew by first name. He related to the young person serving ice cream at McDonalds' with the same level of attention he would as someone with notoriety in town. He was gentle and saw the best in people and situations. The topics he wrote about and the subjects he photographed related to the average person in town.

And that is what made Martin so exceptional. His industry and unpretentious personality gave voice and honor to what others deemed ordinary and unworthy of celebration. We need caring people to help us see the intrinsic beauty and value of every day life. We needed Martin to be with us and yet apart so that he could respond to the cadence and syncopation of rhythms that at first seemed contradictory and tense.

We needed him to help us to stop, consider and find meaning in the routines of life. Martin marched to the beat of a different drum, but it was the cacophony of sounds that his town, state and nation provided him. Now we can reciprocate as friends do, by listening and learning from him.

AN EXPRESSION OF APPRECIATION

If Martin were writing this expression it would be as long as one of the books of the trilogy. It would include grandparents down to grandchildren, and every family person in between. It would include those whose eulogies have been presented in the third volume of the trilogy. It would include teachers, professors and students related to his formal education along with those who aided him in his cultural learning. It would include those who participated with him musically, or over a cup of coffee, or in camp activities and particularly those who aided him in his medical battles. Every fishing buddy, along with every hunting buddy along with every 'gatherer' would be included. It would include every citizen, or clan member, Raven or Eagle, of Sitka, a unique city located in Southeastern Alaska, the beauty of which can not be equaled. Martin was never exclusive.

As the editor I would like to thank Marcia for her long hours of search for his writings, his pictures and her holding together of the family. Our thanks is extended to James Poulson for the picture of Martin, to Henrietta VanMaanen, to Dawn McAllister, proof-reader and occasional editor, and to Dick and Judy Marcum for their technical computer skills. And I extend to God thanks for the ability to put Martin's thoughts together in these books.

Sincerely, Ken Smith, editor.

Contents

THE INTRODUCTION

BUILDING OF THE BOOK

Like a fish out of water I struggle to breathe the breath of purpose.
The possibility of my poetic work to reach a larger audience
Has a strangeness of feeling that it might eventually happen.
It never was my intention to put out a book of my work.
That there are so many hoops I have to jump through is confusing to me.

I can see the value in such a project for my family and friends.
I wonder what universal appeal my work could express to others?
What in my poetic attitude would others see of value?
Most of my effort is written on the same day of the event.
The writing comes easily knowing great people I know.

Being a 'memorial poet' is perhaps what I do best.
I rarely write about my own condition but feelings about others.
I am not one to think on my feet as I have to taste my words.
I get messages from my Tribal elders for reading my poems.
They seem to think I should be more spontaneous expressing myself.

In the beginning of the day I want to be original in my speaking.
The people I meet in my travels deserve something new.
I try to formulate something different in every day greetings.
"How are you?" they ask.
"Fair to poor with gusts to disgusting" is my quick reply.

A dramatic life appeals to me in meeting friends and others.
Why not add something extra special in our daily walk?
My mentors have played an important part in my life.
I will speak in colorful ways without current vulgarity,
Lots of reading sparks my communication skills.

In my formative years I excelled in speech and music.
Missionary contacts lead the way to long for excellence.
Perhaps, involvement in my church taught me to speak well.
Radio and TV work caused me to learn great habits.
It was a continuous learning journey I learned to love.

A long list of mentors paved the way to my eventual work.
Every success I had gathered much praise from my Elders.
My church, in not so subtle ways, guided me forward.
Mother Lila, highly educated, gave me the inspiration I needed.
She exposed me to the world's finest piano music.

I often think of my life as a whole city.
My precincts of thought wander down streets and alleys
Filling my mind of poetic thoughts on a daily basis.
I can scarcely leave my front door without capturing a picture.
My camera, an extension of my mind reaches outward.

There is a question about the camera images I make.
It is in an historical nature I photograph the passing scenes.
The daily changes that move from season to season thrill me.
This year, sadly, I missed the important shore bird migration.
So tuned to Nature this is part of my life style.

The poetic side of images gather in my dreams so often.
In picture and word they visit my life constantly.
I often wonder if I am wordsmith or camera man.
If I am to publish my work which one will be dominant?
Can I combine the two efforts into one publication?
These are some of my thoughts flashing past my mind today.

Your help, dear reader, is much appreciated by Marcia and myself.
I have many questions about making initial efforts in this regard.
The machinery of it all attacks my mind in urgent ways.
But it is a bright ray of hope in presenting my work.

Bridge from Japonski

CHAPTER 1 FAMILY PERSPECTIVE

RALPH'S STORY
April 20, 2006

Listen to me, I have a story of long ago.
It is early Fall and the sea had a restlessness.
The canoe was a worthy craft passed from generations.
The people moved the canoe effortlessly along.
It had seen seasons to travel from Hoonah.

He who gauged the speed, calling out the cadence.
It was not "battle speed" and somewhat less.
The seasoned crew responded to the Tlingit commands.
There were familiar rest stops along the way.
A time to refresh with water and fresh fish.

We are taking young Ralph to what is called school!
The missionaries speak well of it and the Great Spirit.
He will learn their ways and we will miss him.
He has great promise to the Tribal ways.
Some did not want him to go to this school.

The Elders met to consider what risks might come.
In their wisdom they gave the trip their blessing.
His uncle, John, would check on his progress later.

He was a skilled uncle in Tlingit arts and life.
He cherished the time he taught young Ralph.

With all the stops, the trip took over two weeks.
They hauled out at the Dog Point fish camp.
They nourished themselves and rested.
And when the time was right they paddled to Sitka.
The people of the Village came out to meet them.

Ralph Young was delivered in due time to the school.
Sheldon Jackson in the 1870s was just starting up.
Ralph's people felt a sense of accomplishment.
They felt something good would come of it.
They would have a good report to Hoonah.

The Southeast winds of Fall blew hard as they left.
But they were seasoned travelers to the communities.
The long trip back had the wind to their back.
The late fall run of salmon was in season.
Deer and seal were abundant, weapons found their mark.

The fury of the storm increased; they advanced with difficulty.
This was not unusual for this time of year.
Perhaps a day from Hoonah, we know the canoe tipped over.
Sadly all were lost--the whole of Ralph's family.
It was weeks before Ralph heard of the disaster.

Alone but with Tribal support Ralph grieved in Sitka
I often wonder how he took the news.
To have his whole family gone all at once.
His Tribal extensions and missionaries now were family.

When the late Fall winds pick up and the seas rise
I grieve alone for what happened so long ago.
It is a mystery that has no end but sadness.
But my grandfather, Ralph Young started a new life.
I celebrate that richness that he left behind.

April 20ᵗʰ in the early hours of the day I composed this story. I was at the Tlingit and Haida Central Council Assembly at the time. It was for the Memorial program 3:30 P. M. Friday. I made arrangements with the chairman of the program but he forgot because of the many components of the Memorial Program.

Gerry Hope held up my poem seconds before the closing prayer and the chairman remembered me as he asked me to come forward. Most of the poem went as I planned with exception of the final stanza. There was so much emotional energy there I almost cried out loud. My voice started to fail and I faltered slightly but finished dramatically.

Several delegates followed me to my chair expressing their appreciation for my work. I had 115 copies made for each delegate and they were pleased. I hope you'll understand more of what really happened to Grandpa Ralph's family in the 1870's.

A FAMILY HISTORY

Gumboot determination: it is but a small sea creature called a chiton that is washed daily by the waves and tide. It holds tenaciously to the rock foundation under water. It is the Title of Southeastern Alaska Regional Health Consortium (SEARHC) book about people that made a difference in health care in our region: "Gumboot Determination."

It is the reason I am writing about my family that in one way or another "made a difference."

In the 1850s the Elders gave their blessing to have young Ralph Young learn the Western ways at a school in Sitka. The blessing was not entirely 100% because some saw Western ways as evil to their way of thinking in the Tlingit village of Hoonah. But the blessing prevailed and Ralph's family prepared to go to Sitka by canoe. They found fair winds traveling to Sitka. I often wondered what Ralph thought about leaving his town on this long journey.

Arriving in Sitka and speaking in Tlingit they released him into the hands of missionaries. They most likely gave him traditional food and encouraged him to do his best. I quote Elder Paul Jackson in what the Elders might have said in leaving Ralph. "They will come in increasingly great numbers (outside cultures). When you have learned their ways come back to defend us."

The fall time winds rose sharply as they readied themselves for the returned canoe trip to Hoonah. Determined to get back to their families they set out hopefully.

They made good time through the narrows and approached Chatham Straights where tide and winds combined in a dangerous condition. Not far into the storm their canoe overturned off shore. I learned just last year that Ralph's mother made it to shore planted an American flag on the beach and left her shoes and returned to the canoe trying to save some of her family.

She died in that heroic effort. Most of Ralph's family perished on that fateful day.

Without family, young Ralph (who spoke little English) embraced his new family of missionaries in Sheldon Jackson School and accepted their faith. He learned to speak well and he also remembered his roots in Tlingit language and extended family. His name was Theuscut of the Raven moiety. A short biography of Ralph Young is given by Mark Jacobs Jr. and Harold Jacobs in Nora and Richard Davenhauer's book about Tlingit Culture.

Equally determined in her life was "Dwee," Elsie Newell Young. She was from Angoon Eagle moiety and Kaagwaantaan. She first married John Newell and when he died in 1940, John's nephew Ralph Young married Elsie. Ralph and Elsie were heavily involved in the Presbyterian Church thereafter. Elsie grew up in Angoon in the traditional Tlingit ways. She was an expert in yellow cedar root baskets, and many of the cedar baskets she made in those early days still exist today.

As a Tlingit girl Elsie also learned food preparation and the dances the women had in their culture. After arriving in Sitka she was hand picked by Governor Brady as part of the housekeeping services at the Governor's mansion. She quickly learned etiquette of properly serving at grand occasions and banquets. This technique she passed on to her children. Over the years she was very active in her church and Sheldon Jackson events. Monday nights she also participated in the Alaska Native Sisterhood (ANS) meetings at the ANB hall. Her husband, Ralph, was one of the Founders of Alaska Native Brotherhood of 1912.

My two Tlingit grandfathers were very determined men. John Newell and Ralph Young found the Chichagoff Gold Mine. The determined part of it was that they had to wait to release news for two years because Natives could not own land in 1908.

Here's that story. John Newell, Ralph Young, and David Price (all Hoonah clan) stopped in Klag Bay to get water as they had traveled long and slowly out of Hoonah on their way to Sitka. As I heard from my mother, John Newell held the boat off shore while Ralph and David went ashore for a drink of water. When they returned John Newell had his turn ashore. Drinking water he noticed sparkling stones in the stream. They took several of them to Sitka and wondered how they could proceed to get a mine going. After two years of meditation, they found a missionary who would break the news about the gold find.

5

DeGroff, a businessman in Sitka gave them start up money. In Robert DeArmond's book about Sitka, it is written that the stones brought in were 75% gold and 25% rock! It was one of the richest veins of gold ever found.

Postscript: The gold money bought 8 year old Lila Newell a piano. It may have traveled from New York around South America, to San Francisco, and finally through Seattle on its way to Sitka. It is now dying in the home of Martin & Marcia Strand. It is hoped that it will be fixed one day.

Other uses of the gold money Ralph Young and John Newell bought land in-between Seattle and SEATAC airport. The bad news it was lost because of unpaid taxes. We could have been millionaires reports Mark Jacobs Jr.

Smoke houses for salmon were a high priority to cultural Tlingit people. Ralph Young helped make 50 of them for the Tribe with some of the gold money. His boat "Smiles" took the necessary supplies to those remote locations around Southeast.

Lila Newell (my mother) grew up to be a talented piano player. She attended Oregon State where she studied music and education and became a teacher. She married Leon Bashore a Frenchman who was at one time chief of police in Sitka. They had one son, John Bashore (my half brother).

An aside story about Lila: Ball room dancing was taking hold in Sitka. The missionaries feared "it could lead to dancing." Tlingit soldiers returning to Sitka brought dancing to our Community House in the Cottages. On hearing this, the missionaries padlocked the building. The Cottage people were so mad, the idea for the Alaska Native Brotherhood hall was first formed, as there would be a meeting place. Katlian, leader of the Kiksádi clan donated land in the Village for the new hall. My mother was one of the rebel band of musicians and played piano for many of the ballroom dances held in the hall. Walter Soboleff was the violin and cornet player at the time. He is approaching 99 years old this year (2007).

Mother Lila was a teacher in the Bureau of Indian Affairs School on Katlian Street. Many elderly Tlingits remember her work. Herb Didrickson remembers her teaching. The building was eventually torn down and the Tribal Longhouse built on that location. I remember my sister Sofia and I would go to Daisy Peter's house where mother's teacher friends would gather once a week to talk over things. Sofia and I would play outside, up and down the stairs to the huge oil drums. Laura Walton, Agnes Peratrovich, Flora Cook and mother were entertained by Daisy. They would be heard laughing about racial goings on in the community. The racism was so transparent, humor seemed to be the appropriate avenue to put it. Of course, they saw all the injustice it brought to Native people.

John Sverra Strand came into the picture with his dad Martinus, and brothers Kaore and Knute Strand. They came to Sitka for king salmon and coho fishing. John took a liking to Lila Newell in the 1930s. Leon Bashore had left Sitka earlier. I was the son of Lila and John Strand. John was a skilled carpenter and fisherman. Also, in Tacoma as a young man of 21 he was foreman of a smelting business. John would treat Kaore his younger brother to lunches and dinners according to stories told to us by Kaore.

I remember mother Lila as a deeply caring mother wanting her children to become intelligent. She was of very slight build possibly because having TB in the 1930's. I was a TB baby and remember the sweaty nights with endless coughing. Right after childbirth, mother was very weak so I was attended to by whom I call my Tribal mother, Flora Williams.

Mother carried her college experience to the grave. She always read books with depth. Historical novels such as Thomas B. Costain and Agatha Christie were her specialty. The old piano was a constant source of joy to her and her daughter Sofia. They would play Rachmaniov, Chopin, and Von Suppe. I think I get my musical appreciation from mother who possibly played great music on the piano while she carried me before birth.

German/English ancestry with equal determination was Marcia Strand. Grundy Center, Iowa was her hometown. Their business was raising corn, hay and other crops by her dad Marcus A Meyer. There were many German farmers that spoke the language. Her mother ruled the farm with great efficiency taking care of all the details. Marcia's brothers Darrell and Milon are in California and Washington State.

Marcia came to Sitka in the 1960s to teach at Sheldon Jackson's Home Economics department. This is where she met her Native companion, cooking lavish lunches and dinners for him and his family. They soon had three brilliant children: Sara Joy, Martina Rae, and Martin Jr. They were the most photographed children in town.

In the summer months they would go to Iowa to visit grandparents Marcus and Arlene (Susy) Meyer. Our children were adored in Iowa. They were allowed to ride farm machinery and go anywhere on the farm. They took side trips to Dike, Marshalltown, and Cedar Falls, etc. Unique "Maidrite" hamburgers were a specialty of Marshalltown. Marcia's aunts and uncles were always included in friendly visits.

It was during these summer visits that Marcia frantically worked on getting her Masters degree in Home Economics/Education. It took several years but she got it. Martin Sr. would visit them there by bus from Seattle. We also made several trips by Canadian National from Rupert, Edmonton, Jasper, Saskatoon, Winnipeg, and to be met in Albert Lea by car riding grandparents. In later years Marcia was hired to Mt. Edgecumbe High School Home Economics department, where she gave her students 110 percent of herself. They were off to Sitka businesses to learn lifestyle work possibilities.

In 1984 the family began "Food the Native Way." The Dog Point Fish camp became our summer effort where I also taught hunting, fishing, and food gathering. Marcia was in on the development of this fruitful project. The determination to succeed carried the Fish Camp to this very year with the help of the founders Robi and John Littlefield.

After Mt. Edgeumbe closed in 1982, Marcia took work in Anchorage in Alaska Employment. Living in Eagle River, I visited there often with Martina and family. Her son Benny Mancil is here today in Anchorage helping the family business.

Marcia is like a gumboot tenaciously hanging on to her life's goals. So determined she came to Anchorage with a broken little toe. I found her writhing in pain on the bed in Sitka with an ice pack. She would not let a broken toe stop her in coming up here. We just found out about the toe yesterday and she will be here long enough to have surgery if needed. The toe break will heal on its own time.

The creme-dela-crème of determination award this week must go to Jasmine the Black schnauzer for heroic duty above and beyond the call of duty. We launch the boat into the lake with Dennis and two girls. As they pulled away from shore Jasmine looked concerned and left out of the action. She paced the shore madly and when they were 100 feet off shore she boldly jumped into the lake with determination to reach the rapidly disappearing boat. Someone on the boat saw her head above water, coming their way. Dennis slowed the boat and made an attempt to pull her aboard. In that effort Jasmine bobbed beneath the lake surface. However, she came up like a cork and Dennis grabbed her aboard. For the rest of the picnic she commanded attention at every effort ever riding the surf board with Denali and swimming with Lila.

There were two dogs one smaller that barked constantly and the other much larger showed fear at Jasmine's presence. Jasmine knows no fear and thinks she is much bigger than she is. After a few controlling barks, everything calmed down for the rest of the day.

My own story had to do with my growing music appreciation and performance. I play a mean C# minor meditation with variations. I listen to the best concert music in chamber music and ensembles.

There is considerable depth in Russian composers. Prokofieff and Shastakovich. I find myself listening to their work constantly when I want to write a creative poem. Since I am a memorial poet their music takes on a serious attitude in helping me express myself.

What I have found about myself is that I must flex my talents often to keep them alive. Writing, piano playing, juggling, balancing biking, wooden whistle making, practicing with the rock sling shot, playing Frisbee-all contribute to my overall being. The seasonal bird migration holds great interest to me and I take advantage of it.

Remembering poetry I have memorized as a boy is still with me. There is joy in loading my own ammunition and practicing at the rifle range with friends. Teaching hunting techniques at Dog Point Fish camp is a specialty. Carving wooden alder whistles always is a crowd pleaser. All this is in addition to my involvement in cultural organizations; Tlingit & Haida Community secretary, Councilman in Alaska Native Brotherhood Camp # 1, and Chairman of the Elders Cultural committee for Sitka Tribes of Alaska (STA). In that regard I am a delegate to a seminar in Oklahoma City in October 22 through 28.

MY NORWEGIAN SIDE

What do I know about my father, John Sverra Strand? He was born in Norway in the town of Aaslunde. He may have come to America at the age of 8. His father, Martinus Strand married Sofia Fredricka Dahal. They had four children: John, Knute, Kaore, and Anna. Martinus came from Norway first and made his way across the country and eventually settled in Tacoma which is the sister city to Aaslunde. Sofia later came to America with the children. Perhaps John and Knute were the only ones born in Norway.

My dad, John, according to Kaore, was smart and as a young man of 21, he worked in a foundry in Tacoma, where he was foreman with 100 men working for him at the age of 21. Kaore told me that he would visit John at his work and John would take him out to lunch or supper in fine eating places. Kaore does not remember my father's middle name "Sverra" and thought it was something else.

In the 1920s to '30s, Martinus made or bought the Sophie II and took his sons to Southeast Alaska fishing each spring and summer. Aunt Anna never came to Alaska in all her years. They were successful fishermen and when I was born, John stayed in Alaska and married Lila Newell who had a son from her first marriage with Leon Bashore, a Frenchman. Their son was named John Bashore. John was loved by my grandfather, John Newell, the original finder of the Chichagof gold mine along with Ralph Young (Newell's nephew).

"Buddy" Bashore, my step brother, enjoyed the outdoors and even attended Sheldon Jackson School. He taught me to hunt and fish Indian River. In 1947, we had an extremely cold winter with eight degrees for about a month. It was so cold, ptarmigan flew into the Sitka area by the hundreds. Buddy and I would shoot them inside the forest near Totem Park and up Indian River. We would bring home a dozen or so on each hunt. Buddy was an expert pistol shot. He had a Marble's 22 caliber long-barreled pistol and shot the ptarmigan in the head every time.

My earliest memories of fishing with my dad was in a double-ended skiff launched from the beach below grandpa Newell's totem selling stall. Dad had a Cutty Hunk linen line and a polished Lunch Strike # 2 gold and silver spoon hook. He would let out the line from the skiff and hold that line in his hand as he rowed forward. When a coho would strike we would pull it in. There were huge schools of coho all the way out to Jamestown Bay and we would catch 20 then turn around and head for home. I was perhaps seven years old at the time.

My dad, John, leased the "Armor" from "Russian Joe Skarras" who had a large house across from Crescent Harbor. When I was fourteen or fifteen I fished Sitka Sound with my father in the spring. We had no sonar or depth finders aboard but had an Iron Mike (device to keep the boat going straight) and a compass to guide us. Early in the season we would go thirty miles off shore looking for birds, and that is where we would let our trolling lines down to fifty-eight fathoms for king salmon. We would catch about fifty and then come home. One time near Salisbury Sound dad had an attack of bursitis and I had to bring the boat through the narrows all the way home and unload the fish at the dock.

The next few years I did not see dad in the spring or summer as he fished constantly. In April he would join his Norwegian friends and go halibut fishing. They would fish for many days without sleeping. I imagine it was tiring work. Their cook was constantly busy keeping up their strength with fine food to keep them awake. I think he fished the "Repeat" a halibut schooner that came up every spring. When dad would come in from a trip we would have lots of fine food for a while. One time he brought a case of canned oysters that became my favorite. Another time he brought a wheel of Roquefort cheese. He paid $22.00 for it. Now it would be near $250.00. It went down really good with Sailor Boy Pilot Bread crackers. One time he came home before the Fourth of July and brought $100.00 worth of fireworks. The whole "cottages" people helped us fire them off deep into the night. Rockets, cherry bombs, fire crackers, roman candles and sparklers lit up the sky way past midnight!

In my early days I barely remember grandpa Martinus Strand coming up to the house. Most of his visits he smelled of strong drink. That was also a part of my father who had a problem with drinking.

Brother Buddy also drank when he returned from the Army. He worked for the Forest Service and I think it extended his life going out of town for two weeks at a time. He loved nature and hunting and fishing and was an expert Marksman with pistol and rifle. At age forty-five he died in a house fire. He returned home after a night of drinking and started to cook something and the food caught fire and got away from him. He most likely fought the fire and it caught him. I was returning from a motorcycle trip South when I saw people in Sitka saying to me, "Sorry about your brother." It was the day of his funeral. Buddy loved our children. He would come to our house at 407 Sawmill and they would sit on his lap and you could see the happiness it gave him.

The last four years of my father's life were perhaps his best. His doctor told him to stop drinking or die. He stopped and made an effort to make his life right. He was hard of hearing most of his life and he finally got a hearing aid. We would hear him laughing in the bedroom as he heard us talking about him. He really appreciated Sofia and me and the things we have done, Sofia with her piano and French horn, and I with my monologues and tuba solos at Music Festivals.

I got a call at Ohio State from my mother and she told me that dad had died. I came home for the funeral. I saw my dad in the coffin with his huge hands of a carpenter and fisherman folded strongly on his chest. Sofia played "None but the Lonely Heart" which has become a traditional musical piece at family funerals ever since. On this Father's Day, these are some of the things I remember about my dad, John Sverra Strand.

Sitka in 1929

THANKSGIVING AT THE COTTAGES

The stew odor filled the room, of coho gaffed by grandpa in Indian River.
It was late November and the smoked deer meat was ready.
The men were out all night getting clams and cockles.
It seems so long ago when we had snow this early.
My dad, John and brother John Bashore hand trolled.

Winter Kings and halibut caught off Totem park froze.
There was some difficulty getting them out to the skiff.
The Superior #5 spoons were still glistening tied to Cutty hunk.
The Daniels helped bring the round bottom above the tide.
They smiled and took the halibut cheerfully given.

John Newell was busy sharpening the filleting knives.
Grandma Elsie took the knives and skillfully prepared the kings.
Newspaper style and soon ready for the smoke house.
The alder wood I de-barked was split and delicious smoke rose.
It would be only a matter of hours for our first taste.

The "Smiles" anchored off shore and brought fresh seal.
Grandpa Ralph brought in the Winchester 52 Sporter ashore.
It served him well for the seal hunting and occasional deer.
15 gallons of clams and cockles the men unloaded.
30 Dungeness crabs rounded out the harvest.

Gilbert and I helped them unload slipping in the snow.
We dreamed of the day when we would hunt and food gather.
Sister Sofia was helping Charlotte and Grandma Elsie.
Auntie Harriet was working over the bucket of clams.
Thanksgiving was coming up and we were ready.

Hammy and Franklin Jacobs took some clams to their mother.
We always shared what we had with Cottage People.
"Connie" Cook sent Lillian over and took some of the harvest.
Flora and Jimmy brought over fresh baked bread.
We took a break from the work to rest and refresh ourselves.

Alden, Arthur and I checked out the pantry for cookies.
Instead, grandma gave us smoked salmon jerky.
We left disappointed but satisfied.

OUR TREE CLIMBING
Around 1948

The big climbing tree above the Manse is forever gone.
It collapsed decades ago and disappeared into nothing.
I remember the happy times of discovery we had.
Long before we found the tree, there were climbing boards.
Someone before us knew the beauty of that tree.

My gaze wanders up there as I bike by now.
There was danger in the rotting climbing boards.
Once one broke as I climbed but I saved myself.
We had to reach a higher rung after that.
It was worth the climb for what we could see.

High up we developed our dreams of the sea.
We saw the crashing waves on Battleship Island.
The kelp line at low tide in muted brown bobbing.
The longing for a craft to take us out to the surf line.
At 10 years old we dreamed of that sea travel.

Cottage people looked small as we swayed in branches.
No one ever noticed our small bodies so high up there.
It was a bit of freedom we enjoyed as a young person.
We looked the other way knowing the dangerous place.
The strong Southeast wind bent the tree several feet.

Somehow we never told our parents about this place.
It seemed to be something we owned not to explain.
No one of our buddies ever fell off or hurt themselves.
Eventually the ladder rungs lost their usefulness.
And we were busy building rafts to conquer the sea.

Our rafts began as crude pieces and later evolved with more study.
The beaches were a wealth of wood and materials.
A few nails and a hammer was all our young minds needed.
Soon some of our structures had cabins out of the rain.
We were ready for more daring expeditions to the Deep.

It began by taking trips around Totem Park beaches.
The military took tons of gravel for building their fortresses.
Huge pools forty feet deep surrounded the park.
We rode the surf on stormy days and paddled the deep pools.
Salmon, trout, and other fish sought refuge in this new location.

With primitive fishing gear we caught fish from our raft's deck.
It was a proud day when we would get a coho aboard.
Humpies were a dime a dozen but a coho was a real prize.

HOW DISTANT IS THE SNOW

Calling for my sleeping hat I lay down for a night's rest.
The single pane windows draw in the cold sharply.
It's not that cold so why should I complain?
I still dream and have dreams and that's adventure to me.
I visit familiar places that are long gone except in my mind.

I still walk through Totem Park as a young boy bright eyed.
The trees were not as thick as they are today.
The squirrels are not as big as they used to be.
Indian River is much bigger when it rains hard at night.
The migrating birds are fewer than they were when I was young.

My earliest walks hand in hand with my dad are not far away.
Our row boat trips to Silver Bay for coho I remember well.
A single Cutty Hunk line played out behind the boat with bait.
We caught two coho by the time we reached Jamestown Bay.
They were jumping well by the entrance to Thimble Berry Bay.

Oh! The fur seal migration was always special in the late fall.
Playing in the water and feeding before their trip north.
They don't stop here anymore and I miss them.
I was 15 years old as my dad, John, rowed into Silver Bay.
We had ten coho by this time and they were biting well.

Dad talked about what it was like to be a Norwegian.
I faintly remember his dad, Martinus, the first.
A sandy haired fisherman with a good business mind.
His sons, John, Kaore, and Knute were here on the Sofia II
The year I was born, John Strand did not return to Tacoma.

A YOUNG PETER SIMPSON
June 2007

Peter returned to Sitka after years away in another Southeast Alaska Town. We were close outdoor friends in the hunting and fishing scene. We cruised the seaside in rafts, climbed the highest trees, and made our own slingshots.

We shared our young lives growing up in the "Cottages."
Peter was always a part of the early days of my life.
It was a continuous time of outdoor adventure in all seasons.
Sledding on Stuart's hill in snow-packed winter was fun.
Swiftly speeding past our Church over the street to the low tide.

Salmon berry sprouts dipped in sugar picked in spring.
The heavy turnout of herring and shore birds by the thousands.
We boys took part in every part of the evolving seasons.
We watched the building of boats at the old boat shop.
We saw the rotting little canoe under the building.

Car tire inner tubes made the best sling shots.
Monkey berry bush had outstanding "Y" handles.
The "Cottage" boys were competitive shooters.
We went to great lengths to find the roundest stones.
Our skillfulness was tried on old cans and shore birds.

Peter, Gilbert and I were best at tree climbing.
One tree above the Manse was one of our favorites.
You could see way out past "Battle-Ship Island" clearly.
We often dreamed of taking a boat out to the islands.
At age ten our crude rafts kept us close to shore.

Peter was an incredible athlete and proved it daily.

With World War II going on we played soldier games.
Out in our bay battle-ships and amphibious airplanes parked.
In Totem Park machine guns were set up by the Army.
We would sneak undetected into "enemy territory."

He attended Sheldon Jackson and I, Sitka High School.
The high jump. Shot put, and foot races Peter entered.
The Sitka Community would come each Spring to the campus.
Our families enjoyed gathering together in sun or rain..
There was a growing beauty in our lifestyles.

A year or two before his parting Peter helped at our Senior Center.
You could imagine the happiness I had seeing him once again.
We talked at length on the directions our lives had gone.
Many times I wished I had visited him in Klawock.
I asked Esther and Charlie many times how he was doing.

He road shotgun on the Meals-on-Wheels van at our Senior Center.
I introduced him proudly to my peers gathered at table # 3.
We come to the Center early to talk about the day's events.
In his quiet way Peter became a part of our elderly group.
I always looked forward to another interesting meeting with him.

The tools of my life lay before me but my memory of Peter is strong.
Our friendship still intact after all those decades away.
We have lived different lives but each life had its own richness.
I feel the healing blanket of support of his entire family today.
I am so honored to be part of this remembrance with you.

DECEMBER VS. JANUARY

The clock's radio woke me this morning promptly at 6. In my dream state my sub-conscience absorbed the latest news. But that wasn't the real dream I had.

It was the house on Kelly Street that showed me memories of my early living. We lived upstairs in two rooms for my first seventeen years. My dream showed me the cupboard and kitchen sink area. I just realized that we had no refrigerator. That's how we lived from day to day. The food we bought or hunted was what we had. If we got something that needed preserving, we had a locker at the Cold Storage Store.

I remember going down there to get deer meat and other things for mother. I'd bring it home and put it on the drainboard of the kitchen sink. The left side of the cupboard had glass windows where we kept the dishes. There were some valuable designed dishes for special dinners and other things. Sometimes Mom, I called her "The Wizard," kept special things there, including grocery money. I just realized that the oil stove was up-stairs and I had to go to the shed and get oil every now and then.

My dad made the shed. I'm stretching my memory about the shed. It was for the Strand belongings. There were clam digging shovels and space for hanging deer. I remember Dad and I shot a doe out of season and had to wait in the woods until dark and hung it in the shed. Dad's tool chest was there, painted blue with his name on it. John S. Strand, proudly painted. His tool chest contents were stolen out at the mill when he died. It was several days after he died in 1958 when someone who worked with him brought the near empty chest.
I felt
bad about it.

A SLICE OF LIFE WITH MARTIN STRAND

At the Thanksgiving Service at the Lutheran Church I presented this essay on the Wednesday before Thanksgiving. I played the Kessler (ancient) organ and Yamaha Synthesizer using 10 voices for the prelude.

Full of thanks am I for the Sitka Lutheran Church.
My Norwegian heritage rests here on my father's side.
Martin the First brought his three sons to Alaska.
John, Knute and Kaore Strand came to Sitka.
The boat was the Sofia II in the 1920s.

Martin the First and Sofia Fredricka Dahl came from Norway.
They settled in the Tacoma area with my father, John was 8 years old.
Many fishing trips to Sitka were made by the Sofia II.
Lila Newell (Kaagwaantaan) and John Sverra Strand married in the 1930s .
I was born in 1935 as a Tlingit/Norwegian.

I remember pastor Nygard when I was a youth.
Fredrick Kneble Lutheran leader is remembered.
The Blessing of the Fleet our family attended in the early years.
The strong baritone voice of Roy Svenson was impressive.
The special Lutefisk dinners are times to remember.

The military of World War II were served at the Lutheran Center.
I was just a boy then but I could see the pride and patriotism.
Men of the Sea would attend Lutheran services.
My Norwegian side were devoted Lutherans in Norway.
I would imagine the Sitka Church was important to them.

The music I play is a meditation in C# minor.
It is dedicated to Sofia Fredricka Dahl and Elsie Newell Young.
My special Norwegian and Tlingit grandmothers.
I also meditate on my Norwegian and Tlingit grandfathers.
I rejoice in this beautiful building that has meant so much to so many.

Some of my thoughts of music and my reasons for playing it:

> My sultry sounding synthesizer wails out a Far Eastern tune.
> I don't know why I'm drawn toward this music.
> It just appears in my mind and I am hopeless to stop it.
> Easy for me to understand the rhythms of ancient music.
> I sway to the beat of the exciting conclusion.

Opening my mind to tone possibilities is the keyboard.
The joy of creating something strange and new.
New options to this piano player increase my thirst.
Every voice suggests a mood, a rhythm, and song.
Now all I have to do is work on written notation.

> I've progressed musically toward more dramatics lately.
> Like life, my musical moods change with the times.
> The tragic beauty of a minor key full of color is displayed.
> The rising crescendo adds meaning and texture to my work.
> As I understand life more, my music is a reflection of it.

Listening to great concert music of the masters guides my life.
So much variety and energy with deep expression fills me fully.
I'm still discovering music that might have an impact in my mind.
Gustov Mahler's symphonies have been a tremendous influence.
It takes time to listen and learn from a great composer.
If I could give some of this knowledge to my grandchildren!

THE SOFT GREEN OF SUMMER
June 23, 2004

Soft yet deeply green the countryside glows with life anew.
It was not so long ago as a boy I looked longingly from my tree top.
Battleship Island high on the horizon in the setting sun.
Green are the islands washed with ocean spray.
My tree sways in the stiff wind and I hang on in wonder.

Sixty feet up carefully climbed using ancient nailed foot pegs.
Part of an old tree house long gone only remains a shadow.
The fresh hemlock cones are near the top of this old broad tree.
We children climbed without fear having never fallen.
It was special for decades and an important part of our lives.

The crude rafts we built to explore our sea built in such haste.
Sometimes falling apart as we launched them from the beach.
But with each failure our adventures took on a new light.
We improved our nail pounding and made things better.
The sea was always waiting for us to explore.

Driftwood from the park beaches gave us our material.

THE HELPING HANDS
June 28, 2004

The house so neglected for so long is breathing a new life!
Tattered ceiling from endless rain damage is skillfully removed.
Helping hands carefully remove the tiles that are dashed to the floor.
The ceiling no longer dripping torture is bone dry.
The roof painting every two years is replaced with the new.

Happy voices echo throughout the house once again.
The spirits of the shadows cower and are replaced
With joyous noises little heard till now.
Each hopeful victory seems that much larger on the horizon.
402 is face lifted in an extreme make-over at last.

The corners of the room now visible give life giving space.
Dreams awaken that were long dormant.
What seemed impossible now is so near to completion.,
We see with more clarity the beautiful gift of space.
It is hard to hold back the tears of joy I feel now.

Things happening with military precision move forward.
The enemy is clutter and is steadfastly taken away.
What was thought as useful on reconsideration is useless.
Sacrifice initially is hard but the greater good had to be.
We are but custodians of these material things.

There still is editing of storage to think about.
Value judgements must be made after things are fixed.
Space considerations are to be carefully prioritized.
Dumpsters must be filled over and over again.
The house will become a well-oiled machine once more.

The sparkle of a new life is just a short distance away.
Tribal extensions will visit us once again.
We will have more time and energy to be creative.
Fully operational ways will speak to us bringing us forward.
We can dream again and we can live again.

HOW SWIFTLY THE DAYS
July 9, 2004

How swiftly the days have passed since the mission began.
The months of planning are behind us long before the first nail
hammered.
The anticipation of the work built up with the passing of time.
Then came the seasons to put things together.
The wondering if this is really coming to pass was raised in our minds.

The joyous fun we had being a family was really worth the journey.
Suddenly the months apart seemed distant to our feelings.
Reliving our past would come up often as we worked.
The children with shining faces graced each moment and so alive.
I enjoyed the way each sang their own song in this complex world.

See our pride every day they came into our home!
Feel the strength of lives well spent with strong purpose.
Lift our hearts with new found meaning full of opportunity.
Bless the day for what it would bring invigorating us all.
Live each moment to its fullest while we are here together.

Reach out to each other finding family history in the making.
Blend our voices to the tasks at hand in a symphony full of helping.
Skillful artistry of putting the house in good repair is what we seek.
The walls vibrate a message long dormant to our minds.
Sing as you never sang before with robin clarity and beauty.

Tearfully we remember our grandparents and how happy they would be.
This is what they would want for us for the good home.
The brilliantly bouncing sound of voices from the furnace room.
These new walls from which I sang an old song.
Rich harmonics echo in and around the house in such pleasure.

The time for our help is all too soon ending as they take the morning flight.
They seemed so happy to be here and contribute to our well-being.
Shelby, Tyler, Cherie, Martin Jr. And Chris and Neal are packing up.
There is sadness at their leaving but joy in what they have done.
The light in our lives burns brightly for them.

Step by step moment by moment improvements miraculously appear.
Water soaked and distorted ceiling tile are dashed to the floor.
I quickly gather them up, bag them and they are whisked away.
The staples that held them are removed professionally.
Ugly water marks on the ceiling are soon gone for good!

Dennis and Benny put 8 x 4 foot dry wall up and are screwed into place.
As if by magic the room suddenly seems so much brighter.
I am so hopeful that things are on their way for the better.
Detailing on the panels are put in place and they are secure.
The house takes a giant leap forward as something wonderful happened.

The talk continues on a high plain by the workers used to such percussion.
Figuring out where to cut for the best results, things are put in place.
Years of getting it right Dennis instructs Benny to do the right moves.
A symphony of activity falls into place that has its own music.
A keen sense of appreciation builds in the grandparents of 402.

It is time for lunch at the Alaska Native Studies lunchroom.
Director Dennis Demmert stops in with words of encouragement.
John Hughes, citizen of the year for Sitka, joins us for seconds.
Ribs with cole slaw salad is the main menu item.
I think of the times I spent at SJ as a young man learning.

Back to the work place and a few more hours of fruitful effort.
My dreams return and seem more possible with each passing hour.
I will be able to expand my horizons with this gift of space!
Yellowed with age wooden tile in the kitchen is taken away.
The dumpster fills for the fifth time and they come to get it.

The front door is taken down in its decrepit state never to return.
The new door jam is carefully placed and adjusted many times.
The door is put in and is fit to perfection and swings clear.
Martin and Neal busy themselves with the new paneling.
Dennis fills the ceiling with dry wall and leaves space for the light.

The ancient piano is witness to all this activity.
First tuned in 1932 by D. A. Sherif the piano tuner of the day.
The piano bought with the first gold money from our mine in
Chichagof.

THE EMPTY VESSEL

Is there a wound that time cannot erase?
Is there a hurt so deep nothing can reach it?
A door opened that cannot be closed?
A future that fades away before reached?
Dark thoughts on the horizon of my life.

A family fractured for the poorest of reasons.
Someone at the controls of life taking it away.
Picking up the fractured pieces so scattered.
The clock ticking bringing no relief.
All the good that was done is now in the shadows.

Just where can the healing begin?
What ray of hope can we expect?
The contact closed almost without warning.
Empty thoughts blowing in the wind.
Who will make the first move?

Can there be pain without pain?
Alone with our feelings stretched to the limit.
The night seems so much longer than before.
The days stretch toward meaningless thoughts.
A ship without a rudder taken by the wind.

I saw my grandchild yesterday at his play.
"Hi! Grandpa!" as my heart lifted briefly.
A little life drawn into a distant understanding.
Longing to hold him close was my first thought.
What would those whose hate is strong say?

Somewhere in Sandy the children play together.
Young minds of Girdwood are growing.
Grandparents seem more distant than before.
Tear drenched pillows fill during the night.
A feeling of emptiness greets our mornings.

The sadness of a Shostakovich quartet drones on.
My writing falters for a painful moment.
The music turns prayerful speaking of slight hope.
Trapped way out on an incoming tide of grief.
Pulling what strength I have left I stop writing.
What is the next move?
What will the Holidays bring?
Will there be letters?
Will the phone ring once again?
Questions pile upon each other without answers.

Beach Park playground

OUR ANCIENT FOUR ZERO SEVEN, SAWMILL HOUSE
August 19, 2006 Sitka

Our ancient 407 Sawmill house now quiet and alone waits for a buyer down the road. Offers have been coming in and we will be selling soon.

O, the memories of that place! Sara Joy banging on her high chair tray. Martina being bathed in the kitchen sink. Martin Jr. Sitting on the lap of his uncle, John, in the front room. Daddy adding another gun to the gun rack. Mother slamming the door as she leaves for the shore boat to work.

Deer hanging in the shed ready for butchering. Coho caught at the rocks of Sheldon Jackson. Our cat draped on Mother's neck as she ate supper. "Little Bit" meowing for my microphone close to the floor. Martina and Sara Joy blowing dandelion seeds on the SJ lawn into the wind. Martin Jr. Weaving his little bike down an icy road. Dad creating another image in the darkroom hoping it is his best yet!

Letters to Santa read on the air by my children. I made Daddy look good around town. Sara Joy and I had our first motorcycle crash at 2 miles on hour on cemetery hill. We cried together as we rode back home. I woke the children up at 2 A.M. on a summer night to watch the big frogs on the road at Swan Lake and brought one home to photograph in the bath tub. We have no more frogs on the lake anymore.

The joy of moving to our new house at 402 Baranof Street. Our back yard and front yard golf course for Martin Jr. and me. The tree sprouts the girls got from the Forest Service and planted in our front and back yard. The front yard 55 gallon steel barrel this year was broken apart by the 35 year old spruce tree the girls planted.

Our kayak trips out to sea and to Blue Lake are remembered. We caught large rainbow trout at the lake. Our picnics out to the islands were special. My brother, John and I went out to the hunting bays. He was the greatest outdoor man I have ever known. Respect for nature he taught me of the ever present dangers. I remember the kayak trip with Martin Jr. To Katlian Bay. We camped inside a circle of logs and it was the biggest rain of the year.

We had a richness of being together in those days. At six weeks old, Sara Joy was taken across Canada by train to Iowa to grandpa Marcus and grandma Arlene (grandpa always called her Susy), Martina and Martin Jr. Had trips to California. 1984 we went to Hoonah and stayed with Buster and Martha and visited at length with Jessie and George Dalton. 1985 we spent Christmas with Angoon and our Tribal relatives. We had another whole new world in the Sitka Native Education program. During the ten years each child took part in that wonderful experience.

Here in Sitka we long for that closeness once again. If there is anything we could do to talk to each other and visit again that would be great. We willingly wait to hear from each of you by letter, phone or e-mail when the time is right for you.

FOUR ZERO TWO BARANOF

Just an expression of joy at having you over to our house to make those beautiful improvements. November saw record rainfall in Sitka. Can you imagine 19 inches in just one month? At night I'd hear heavy rain and a shudder of horror would pass though my mind thinking I heard a leaking roof. A flashlight to the ceiling would reveal NO LEAK, it was just water making sounds in the hot water pipes!

We remember with pleasure our new ceiling being put in place with the help of Dennis assisted by Benny holding up the sheet rock. My boy, Martin was quick with a helping hand wherever needed.

Cherie helping to prepare the next portion of the project keeping Tyler and Shelby focused with a dash of good humor. Cherie and Chris applied buckets of paint to the walls with the confidence of professionals. It was good of Neal to work on the detail work on the doors and walls. Gradually the home where Sara Joy, Martina Rae, and Martin Jr. earlier lived took on a new look bringing a tear of joy to the eyes of their parents.

Lila brought her personality forward with her command of the language to the delight of everyone. Camera woman, Marcia, photographed with merriment Denali and Shelby who tried to dodge the camera often. Tyler worked tirelessly outside painting the skirting around the house, green. When it was clean up time grandma Marcia handed him some 1960s sheets of soap to wash his hands and that brought a laugh from him. Tyler and Shelby enjoyed cousin Gary and took every opportunity to play with him. Mike Roberts charter boat the "Tackle Box" gave us an incredible outdoor experience. The successful fishing was enjoyed by all aboard. And it was generous of him to take us out on a second trip!

The boat trip to the hatchery was one of the highlights of our gathering! The ancient Indian art of cooking king salmon with an open fire was impressive. Tyler set a new record in watermelon eating,to his delight. Grandma Marcia helped Gary with his baked potato and he expressed pleasure finishing his plate of salmon with expertise. Grandpa Martin looked longingly at the king salmon swimming in the holding pond and wished he had his salmon rod.

Sara and Bill provided excellent housing for the family and how could we forget that splendid BBQ? We enjoyed getting the various lunches around town and at Sheldon Jackson College. A lot of water has run under the bridge since those happy times together. Our memories are strong about all we accomplished at 402 Baranof!

Marcia and I appreciate all the help and fellowship you brought us. Somewhere down the line we hope you can find it in your hearts to forgive any problems we may have created. Here's hoping you all have rich, meaningful lives free of harmful addictions. Thankful for your help we are.

COTTAGES

Saintly elders visit upon my mind within the life I've lived.
"The Cottages" environment where thoughts of ANB and ANS
reside.
Leads light into the dark days the Tribe has known.
Meditation with purpose during the long walk to ANB Hall.
The agenda is about grandchildren given a fair chance.

Ralph and Elsie Young, walk closely together along Crescent shore.
Clutching a small jar of soap berries Elsie moves forward.
Ralph, with some trolling money, for someone to go to Washington.
A handshake for both of them from Andrew Hope at the Hall.
The meeting will begin within a half hour; they greet neighbors.

The Cottage band is assembling up front at the stage.
Conductor Alfred Gordon busies himself passing out music.
Walter Soboleff is asked to tune up the band.
Soon over 100 members gather bringing the finest food from the sea.
Seal stew is the crowds's favorite along with smoked deer meat.

Paul Liberty moves forward and gives a prayer with deep feeling.
The band plays the fight song, "Onward Christian Soldiers."
The people settle down to a lavish dinner, the first of the season.
The young children scurry around playfully and secure.
The elders smile at the beauty of their children and future.

Practicing at night after food gathering in the summer the band
Is once again complete and ready for this opening night.
"The William Tell Overture" is played with much spirit.
Thunderous applause at the ending and the crowd stands.
We are musical people and as Tlingits perform beautifully.

Roberts Rules of Order takes command of the meeting.
The ANB and ANS Presidents guide and listen to the people.
The issues are discussed in detail and everyone given a chance to speak.
Then a break for delicious soap berry dessert from a huge bowl.
Grandma Elsie Young prepared it and smiles broadly.

The meeting ends late into the night and the members are tired.
Looking forward to another day they leave refreshed.
We are making progress fitting into a strange new world.
The dream of our Founders is advanced another day.
A light rain follows us back to the "Cottages."

TO BE YOUNG IN SITKA

A boy of seven could hardly wait for them to bite.
Gilbert and I came home with six for the frying pan.

The lure of the sea came early in my life and the life of others.
Experimental craft were put together but un-seaworthy.
A sudden wave and we were often dumped in the shallows.
We were very wise, testing our work in the shallows.
Hammer and nails were put to good use on the shore.

Paddles and poke poles propelled our crafts.
In dangerous deep water the paddles were superior.
More streamlined rafts were made, some with cabins.
This was a luxury in rainy weather and crashing waves.
My outrigger raft was the fastest of the fleet.

Young salmon berry sprouts came up and we ate them.
Slightly sweet taste and refreshing to us all.
The tall trees behind the Manse we climbed looking seaward.
The first ten feet was the most difficult for toe and hand placement.
The reward was a high look out to "Battleship Island."
The "Cottage" children would have a longest day march up Indian
River.
We would start around 8 P. M. and walk until deep shadows came.
No bears ever bothered ten or twelve of us young ones.
Sometimes we would start a fire along the river after drinking water.
Then it was hide and seek all the way back home.

THESE EARLIEST THOUGHTS
Around 1937

Using the strength I have been withholding
I meet the hidden danger that has been lurking.
More than once it came from the dark side of life.
Molding the collection of various fears come forward.
The earliest dream of dread while I was still in my crib.

Like great seaweed in deepest sea the wind sways the curtains.
I felt something strange hovering over my childhood bed.
There was a living evil I cannot describe alive then.
Years later I visit my dream like state once again.
A chill runs through my bones just at the thought of it.

These earliest thoughts give a feeling of uncertainty.
Awakened during the night a cold sweat pours out.
It is as if I dare not turn around to meet this fear.
It is winter time, the time for dark thoughts.
When the blackness of night gives no answers.

I have learned to overcome this unusual life form.
So far it has done no great harm but someday it might.
It is like a great book being written page by page.
The turns and surprises burning from a fresh source.
The urging time I must write it down in detail.

The mystery continues as I write poetry of early times.
The rhyme, meter, and musical forms come together to
Show a moment in time beating away at eventide.
What a Devine visit from brain to fingertips.
The finished product leaps forward to the page.

The elegy I play in its sadness minor key blossoms.
Excitement as I visualize what I have done this night.
Alone with my piano talking to me of ancient times.
Way past midnight words building to something good.
Asleep in the chair I find myself in earliest morning.

The sweetest bird songs outside my window awake me.
The varied thrush in its soft trill is united with
The red breasted robin's glissando to the highest note.
The evening wren is telling all of its territory.
The perfumed cedar fills the country side gloriously.

I look over the opportunities of the day carefully.
Keeping my curious eye alert for picture possibilities.
I fill the frame with the Sitka rose in brilliant red.
Rich green detailed leaves softened with morning dew.
The soaring raven, wings outspread lands at my feet.

The silver lure flies through the air in a large arch.
Delicate splash in the ocean shallows twists and turns.
Noticed quickly by the trout the attack begins.
A sizable fish fights for its life and gives it to me.
Silver, with speckled back and pink line down the sides.

Soon I am not alone on SJS rocks as others fish with me.
Our families praise our efforts that are cooked for dinner.
Grandmother saves some fish for the smokehouse that day.
My thirteenth year has its own happiness living off the land.
I learn to give to the Elders what I have caught and am all smiles.

WRITING WITH MEANING

March 29th I repaired "Back Door" Becky's Canon AE-1 camera and was paid $62.00. She still has my 50 mm for lens which I should charge $60.00. David led me on that he wanted my Pentax H1 but when it came to pay the money he said he had none. He gave me an Olympus 50 mm 1.4 lens and I told him he had $25.00 down on his next purchase. I was somewhat disappointed that the deal fell through!

On April 3rd I turned 58 years old. Sara and Robert had a birthday cake for Marcia and me. Both of my parents died at age 58. We'll see if I can make it to 59! I ought to be good for at least a couple more good years.

Right after Easter Sunday I went to Juneau for the Tlingit & Haida Assembly on April 14th though 17th. I took my Minolta 110 Zoom camera with me and it worked beautifully. A Tribal sister, Nancy Hansen from Petersburg, met me there and we talked about our other Kaagwaantaan relatives in Southeast Alaska. The Assembly was a rich experience for us all. I will have to campaign in early 1994.

Before April 19th, Sara Joy talked with one of her workers, about having me do her wedding pictures. On April 24th, I met with Cheryl and Tom and they agreed I should do the wedding and put $100.00 down. The wedding is for May 8th

Looking through the records of the Cottage Women's Society from 1902 to 1927, I am sad by the lack of reporting of Indian doings around town and Southeastern Indian communities. During the early years the minutes of the Society were scribed by several secretaries including my Grandmother Elsie and later my Mother, Lila Newell Bashore Strand. There was no mention of the upcoming Potlatch of 1904. No reference was made to the new sleeping giant, the Alaska Native Brotherhood and Sisterhood. There was no reference to the trips to ANB-ANS conventions that had very good attendance at that time. Perhaps, the "Tlingit" newspaper at that time would give more about Indian society activity. In my casual look at this newspaper I found more about the Cottages than the <u>Verstovian</u> revealed. There was much mention of the church's mission to other countries and our nation. It was like being in a news black-out where only hymns and scripture and things of the church mattered.

It would have been wonderful to hear about the seasons and their changes and harvest for food. I would have been happy to hear that Indian hunters came up the beach with twelve deer and four seal for the coming Potlatch.

The common thing I found in the church records about the Cottage Women's Society was the good English usage of each secretary. They seemed comfortable writing long, important sentences and being able to express themselves well. I think I know why it was possible to get such highly educated women to learn the English language so quickly. It was the church's policy that the students not speak their Native tongue. By doing this they could learn the Western ways much more quickly. It was a high price to pay at the expense of their Culture. I'm told that the elders of the Tribe wanted it this way. They could see the new culture coming and embraced Christianity as a way to save the Tribe and educate the young in new ways.

I've come to know and expect musicianship excellence, devotion to the Almighty, dependence on God's natural provisions of fish, deer, and berries; active participation in politics and the fight for the right to vote and own land. That's what I've learned by living in the household of Elsie Newell, Tlingit woman of Sitka, Alaska. I'm the upright grand Kohler and Campbell piano and have lived with the Newell family since I was young.

Freshly smoked salmon, rendered seal oil, and wild berries are on the table ready for eating. Young and old voices were back in the house after a summer at fish camp where the year's food was gathered, preserved, and prepared. This was my favorite time of year when Lila and her sister Harriet returned to converse with me on my keyboard.

TODAY WE REMEMBER

They sing their way to freedom.
Their music had such soul knowing the pain they surely knew.
We sing heavy with remembrance for Dr. King.
He spoke the poetry of a hopeful life ahead.
The music of his words resounded throughout the Nation.

The transparent hate even reached the shores of Sitka,
The great fear that minorities "might succeed" was the danger.
Auntie Helen took us to the movies when I was 5 year old.
And we sat in the section that the society of the day said Indians were
to sit.

Our church and Tlingit Elders cheered us on to be excellent.
That was the encouragement we needed to move forward.
The unjust racial climate continued horrifically everywhere.
We sang, hoped, and prayed that it would end soon.
It lasted too long for our young minds to understand.

We were no strangers to racial prejudice ourselves.
My grandfather, John Newell died when I was 5,
The same year my new grandfather, Ralph Young heard
Word from Juneau that Elizabeth Peratrovich took
A giant step forward for Alaska Civil Rights.

It was a dark day in my life at the death of Martin Luther King.
As I broadcast the news on radio an empty feeling
Came over me of so eloquent a spokesman for the cause.
It was as if the lights went dim over our world.
Mahalia Jackson's depth of sadness sang for us all.

It is good to see Sitka's creative art for this day.
What a valuable program we have to remember.
Our art, words, and music is a fitting tribute to the
Struggle Dr. King lead the Nation.
I am glad that you called on me for this important event.

CHILD'S PLAY, TOO

People suffer without imagination,
I would be so empty in my life without it.
It has to be used everyday to keep in shape.
That is what made radio so very special.
To have the mind examine life in many ways.

It is my season to give back the imagination I have taken
Return the beauty and wisdom that has moved my life.
It took a long time to realize what I had to offer.
I work with words, music and pictures.
It is time for me to display my talents.

For the past 3 years I have taken every opportunity to speak.
I have written memorials and special essays in public.
Inspiration comes to me so easy knowing good people,
People that moved me emotionally in one way or another.
My failing mind still remembers great details of the past.

The shorebird migration is once again history for Sitka,
Great varieties of birds came here in better numbers.
Memorable among them is the Greater White-Fronted geese.
As a youth I hunted them on their Northern journey.
The elders and my family loved their great taste.

Today I visited the "Cottages" where I lived.
The old house on Kelly Street faced the sea proudly.
Down on the beach where we brought in deer and seal.
I remembered the weathered bullhead rock pools.
Newell, Young, Jones and Anderson boat landing is there.

The warm May tide creeps rapidly up the flats with light wind.

Found stones for my sling arched high and splashed.
Oh! The birds I hunted were coming in the thousands.
The plaintive cry of the Old Squaw ducks late into the Spring night.
My eyes wet with joyous tears facing the sea.

Standing on the rocks to the West I caught coho.
10 years ago and longer they came every Fall.
Huge schools of Dolly Varden came after World War II,
Dad and I would catch 20 each before coming home.
40 foot deep pools where the Navy took gravel for their work.

A piece of string, a bent common pin, and a worm for my first
fishing,
Pan sized rainbows under the bridges would bite.
Patience waiting for them to take the bite.

LOOKING TOWARDS OCTOBER

Thundering rain of the day beats on the roof as I take
A deep look at my life so far. What meaning have I
Brought to others around me? What contribution did
I give to my fellow man? With the time I have left
What can I reasonably do to help others? There seems
So little time remaining.

My attitude tonight is colored in reflective music of
Tchaikovsky's "Pathetique" symphony number 6 in B
Minor. When a Russian president dies it is the music
Played at the funeral. It is heavy with sadness but
With much beauty of a life well lived in service to
Others. It very well expresses my thoughts of my life.
I have had a rich life and have experienced beauty.

In my small way I have carried the torch forward for
My tribe. I have not been deeply involved as I should
Have been. I would have loved to speak Tlingit and
Dance with confidence with my Kaagwaantaan
Members. Maybe, my willing spirit is enough being
An advocate of cultural things? There is so much to
Be done and my tools are so few.

It was such a thrill to be involved in the Totem
Raising Friday afternoon. The biggest story was
Missed in the press. The entire enrollment of Mt.
Edgecumbe was there along with Pacific High.
Some Sitka students were there also but not as many.
I was proud that the young take an interest in this
Most precious moment in Sitka history. The rain was
Steady but the spirit of the ceremony was not

Dampened at all. The Kiksádi clan was enlivened in
Giving Katlian his historic right. Clan witnesses
Beamed in the grayness of the day with heads held
High for the event.

THE WORLD OF LIBRARIANS

With a nation screaming for literacy I invade the life of librarians.
I, egocentric broadcaster, wordsmith am taken aback in awe.
A peek into this other lifestyle I see and feel the beauty before me.
A life of determination and dedication shows its working face.
Caring, articulate museum people; surround me with their high goals.

With lives sharply focused, intent on serving their people, I feel as
Intruder, empty and longing to be filled with their kind of hope.
Listening intently with our group I am looking for new standards.
Inspiration in my learning ways builds with much appreciation.
Today, I am enriched and growing with so much caring help.

The rain soaked bus rides into the morning strong with purpose.
Strangers become friends, talk across the aisles as smiles broaden.
I speak in good humor to my new neighbor about my life.
We pass two Native casinos and ancient urges sweep my mind.
This gamble of life has a partner, out there blinking its light.

They ganged up on us, those experts in the field of helping others.
I reached into my college life pulling out what skills I could muster.
Alien after years of little study, my mind unwinds of remembered times.
When thinking was so sharp and work of the day so right for the moment.
Poor is the Nation that has no heroes. Disgraceful are those who forget.

I look to our Elders' language to the future generations.
Preserving their writing and oratory is our task today.
Reel-to-reel voices of another time jump into our lives joyously.
Our ancient ancestors speak to us again trying to show us the way.
The research continues to bear fruit as our work moves forward.

Cinnamon sticks fuel our meeting into the night brings us joy.
Learning our personal journeys we laugh and become closer.
Everything is working for our benefit and our eyes sparkle.
Into the gathering night we move on to our resting places.
There is another morning of opportunity tomorrow for life!

CHRISTMAS EVE AT THE COTTAGES
2005

Today I met with my mother Lila, my dad John, my brother Buddy and we had a good talk. I relived all those Christmas times of my early childhood. The smell of mince meat pie drifted up the stairs of 102 Kelly street as grandma Elsie cooked four large, thick pies.

A large pot of smoked dry fish with potatoes was on the top of the stove and we all knew our lunch meal would soon be done. Grandpa Ralph yelled up the stairs for us to come down. Charlotte and Edith brought Jean down from the other room. They were giggling girl talk all the way down the stairs. I slid down the Cedar dark wood stair railing.

Grandma Elsie's living room was large with warm loving artwork on the walls. The piano had cedar root baskets and small totems carved by John Newell, my first grandfather. There was a glass display case with white and blue Chinese plates and bowls.

Facing the Southeast, the windows brought in the faint December light. We could see the ocean and boats passing. Seagulls, ravens, ducks, and geese could be clearly seen. Earlier in the year from our upstairs window I shot my 22 rifle across the road and down the beach. Six large geese were 125 yards down on the sandy spot. I held the rifle one foot high, squeezed the trigger and the bullet found its mark.

But today was Christmas Eve and we had Dad's favorite Holiday meal, roast deer meat roll. It was lightly spread with spices as he rolled it in fat and meat. This was taken downstairs and this was one of uncle Gibson Young's favorite meals.

Roscoe and Harriet Max came in and Auntie Harriet brought in a spice cake she had made. Grandma Elsie had me go out to the smoke house and bring two smoked hind quarters of deer that were ready. Adding salt and pepper they went into the wood stove oven. Jessie and Frank Price came over and talked of plans for the Christmas eve service tonight.

Jenny and Lars Anderson knocked on the front door bringing Haines soap berries for dessert.

Their daughters Hazel and Ester giggled with Jean and Charlotte out on the porch. Sofia joined them later after she practiced on our piano that my grandfather bought for his daughter. I have that piano today.

The living room table was huge and grandma Elsie put part of her history to work. She had worked in Governor Brady's mansion on Katlean street so she knew how to set up a table for a banquet. The plates and silverware were arranged with care, serving spoons at the correct angle.

Grandpa Ralph took a reflective moment and opened with prayer. There was deep commitment in his strong voice as he remembered those family members who could not be here. It then was time for the main event. Charlotte, Edith, and Jean brought out the harvest from the kitchen and placed them on the table. And we enjoyed each others company.

After dinner my mother Lila played the "Spinning Wheel" with great applause. Sister Sofia (Fia) played Christmas Carols she had learned last year and we all sang.

Flora and Jimmy Williams stopped by to give us greetings and they brought Clarence, Elinor, Sylvia, Marta, Willy, and Jimmy boy. Soon Mark and Annie Jacobs came over with Harvey, Ernie, Hammy, Franklin, Bertha, Mark Jr. and Rosie. Esther and Charlie Littlefield came in the back door and sampled the goodies and wished us Merry Christmas.

It was now time for our Church Christmas Eve Service and we all walked over to the church on the Sheldon Jackson Campus. The Messiah was sung that evening.

SITKA HIGH WE WILL FIGHT FOR THEE

My security blanket is warm again for another reunion.
My peers are here with their smiling faces.
The years of longing to be with them is over tonight.
Names long neglected in memory flash to attention.
Theirs is the beauty of long ago giving me a blessing.

Our mighty "Prince" remembers us well as if yesterday.
The music of his life shines as if he never left us.
I started playing my tuba after 40 years of dust gathering.
Remembering our conductor's enthusiasm to teach us.
I recalled all the fingerings on my horn and played on.

We, like salmon returning to its birth stream we come.
Battle worn and tarnished we are the glorious survivors.
We give a big smile at those stories of long ago.
The sincere embraces warm up the whole room.
Reunited for a short but meaningful time we are here.

Sitka High breathes a new life of beautiful lives.
Things left unsaid are said now with conviction.
We realize how important we are to each other.
The planners of this event know they've got a winner.
The tears of joy are everywhere tonight.

We talk of those gone but not forgotten loved ones.
Memory moments gather in our minds.
Sitka, where our fears and dreams collide we talk.
Growing up in such a setting building our lives.
Thankful for the great teachers in our passing parade.

Soon we will part once again, but knowing the joy we have.
Back to our far-flung dreams around the Nation.
Pictures, words, and wonderful memories are going with us.
Long, lingering goodbyes at the airport a little tearful.
We're from Sitka High this is the banner we carry.

MARTIN R. STRAND
KAAGWAANTAAN EAGLE'S NEST HOUSE
KWÁCH SITKA CAMP #1

Share with me the pride I wear today looking out into the lives around me.
This is the forum grandpa Ralph Young enjoyed and took so seriously throughout his life.
Today I feel the strength in numbers toward our cause.
I celebrate the lives of Ralph and Elsie Young.

They were always near and never distant in any way.
There was an urgency in their teaching us the way to do.
God, culture, and family were the priorities of the day.
They were quick to reward good behavior.
Taking me deep into Nature was a good part of their mission.

I was privileged to have spent two magical harvest years with them at Nakawsina Bay fish camp.
At eight and nine I would hear the wonder of the roar of fish jumping loudly into the night.
It is a sound that I would never hear again.
We were taught to take care of ourselves on land and sea.
In the morning we would catch the fish.
In the afternoon the women would pick berries.
Oh! The Tlingit songs of the women in the salmon berry field.
Fish heads, backbones, and tails were cooked to perfection each evening.

The rain was never threatening to us as we continued our work.
The depth of sensitivity of grandpa Ralph's prayers
Included those we left behind away from camp and the
ancestors that fished and camped here.
It was Fall time with crab apple tree leaves turning golden.

This is what I learned from my grand parents so long ago.

BUILDING A CAREER
Velma Baines retires after many years work. May 19th, 2006

Catching the shore boat *Arrowhead* she goes to town.
Charlie Littlefield invites her aboard with his gentlemanly smile.
Seagulls hover behind the boat as they leave Sitka.
A Southeasterly wind blows rain into the craft.
Two sea lions curiously swim a cautious distance.

A newly wed Home Economics teacher joins Velma.
They engage a lively conversation as the boat rocks.
John Luke and Johnny Hope are also aboard just off work.
As they round the bend, the shore boat *Donna* passes.
Ruby Gossett sits quietly in the back of the boat.

There is talk of building a bridge to Japonski Island.
So far it is only a dream but a persistent one.
Velma busies herself preparing the salad of the day.
The handsome Louis Minard is chopping the steaks.
Matthew Williams is getting the oven ready.

The Baines children are running all over the island.
Their father is out fishing with the Mosquito Fleet.
Joe Peterson just got his glorious new cabin cruiser.
Charcoal island and Millerville house the people.
The motor vessel *Mt. Edgecumbe* is arriving with students.

Decades of change gradually come here.
The bridge was built, the airport was at last a reality.
The Baines family moved to their Wolf Drive home.
Velma continued her career at the hospital
She swims today in a bright stream of praise.

This gathering of friends unite to wish her well.
She has an active life ahead of her.
We will be cheering every success along the way.
Her rich, full life speaks volumes of good.
We join her supportive family wishing every happiness.

CLOSING ANOTHER YEAR, 2006

A night to remember in December 2006. I am going to try to carefully gather all the details of what happened as I listen to Fantasia on a theme of Thomas Tallis by Vaughn Williams. A raining winter day about 10 P.M., when I heard voices outside. It was the fire department men trying to control a blaze developing at the Red Finch house next door. The flames were gathering around the skirting of the house and building. Fortunately, there was little wind from the Southeast and the flames engulfed that house.

My life flashed before me and I thought, Marcia should know about this so I called her at work. She seemed calm as I asked her what I should save in case our house caught fire. It was a stubborn fire deep under the building. The men removed the skirting and hacked through the floor while spraying with water. Finally it was under control. The lady next door was safe but the house must have been a mess with all that water damage. The men had to tear down our fence which ran right up to the house.

My will to photograph was long gone and I just looked on in disbelief. My thinking was, "what should I try to save from our house" I thought of all the things that we have saved for our family. My prints and negatives, Marcia's mementos from the cradle to our children's teen years. Our ancient piano that some day will be passed on to whoever wants it. My cameras and lenses and accessories and my computers and my written work are important. Dangerous chemicals and gun powder are upstairs.

I thought of how temporary our things and lives are. We must share what we have where it will do the most good. We have been shameless recyclers who collected and hoarded and never gave anything away. I am trying to look at what I have but not used in the past five or ten years. We have to move on while we still can. In 2007 I want to make a list of all the things I have and if there is value pass it on to someone who can use it. I have been blessed as a photographer to have such good equipment. As the months and years pass they are becoming obsolete and dying because they are not used.

A good note: I have been burning (recording) music from my CD library which is in good shape. You will be receiving CD's and DVD's from my collection. My first recording project is to record music that has been part of the Strand history. Music my mother loved and harmonica music dad enjoyed. Music Sofia played on the piano and organ. Music I played on tuba at music festivals. Our wedding music in 1962. Band music of the Cottage band from the 1920s. Sheldon Jackson operettas and choir music. The first music I played on "College Concert" in 1953 at KSEW. Marcia has countless videos taken by her of our family and travels. I am getting into position to edit video.

LOWER FORTY-EIGHT FAMILY

The generosity of the Martin Strand Jr. Family brightened our day. We had been away so long in Alaska it was good to be with our Gresham family once again. Tyler and Shelby had grown into vital young people. Their dedication to their swimming program reminded me of our children with their early morning practices at Blatchey Pool. Cherie devotedly made sure they were on time for their events and Martin Jr. was there for them. We made a side trip from Gresham to Portland by Mass Express. It was our taste of big city living.

Arriving in Seattle we took an Express Van directly to Sofia's place. The van driver used GPS all the way to the exact spot on the map. Sofia and Julie gave us a warm welcome and we caught up on family business. Sofia's limousine service was outstanding. I brought her my Sitka Community band concerts of 2003 and 2004. It was my first attempt to copy CD's to share. We would listen to them while driving to Virginia Mason hospital.

My evaluation tests began with 16 vials of my blood. You know what a coward I am when it comes to needles. There were about a dozen doctors and specialists looking over me. I have polycystic kidney disease. Yes, they are weak but working-the kidneys, that is. Down the road they might need more attention. Oh! Before I forget while in Portland I sprained my back getting into my briefs. If that was not enough I brought flu-like symptoms from Alaska and with it ice cream headaches. I could not do my treadmill test because of the back so they gave me a chemical stress test. I nearly fainted during the preparation needling. But I came through alright. The test noticed a 30% problem with my heart but 70% looked good. Two days later the doctors wanted to do the treadmill test and I agreed. That test showed another heart problem and the doctors agreed that the testing was inconclusive. And that's where I stand today. I may be taking a trip to Anchorage in a month or so for further work. I'm feeling fine.

As a child age three and earlier I had TB. Last September I tested positive for the TB. Once you test positive you always will be positive. They are giving me a daily pill that would clear up my body from any remaining TB.

We had lunch at the Seattle Indian Senior Center with Sofia. We also took in the Gresham Senior Center earlier. Sofia goes there often and introduced us to her friends. They want me to send them herring eggs in April.

We left Seattle heading to Sitka, but all planes were canceled when we hit the ground in Ketchikan. A vast snow area the size of Rhode Island hovered over Sitka and Juneau. We stayed at the Gilmore Hotel as distressed travelers at a reduced rate of $66.00. The next day we hauled our belongings to the ferry boat that goes to the airport. It was snowy and slippery and windy. It was real torture hauling our luggage up and down the slippery gang planks--twice that day! In the afternoon we got on the plane and flew over Sitka and Juneau and headed to Anchorage where we had two good days visiting our grandchildren Benny, Lila, and Denali. Sitka did not look good when we finally boarded the 9 P.M. flight.

CHARLES & MARION
Snail House purchased by S. J. Professor

I am so enriched by our visit to your new house in Hoonah! The courtesy you extended to me was outstanding. It was the most valuable of the 36 goals I had to accomplish in Hoonah. I treasure the fragment of a dish from the 1944 fire.

You were mentioned in my Convention report to Sitka Camp # 1, when I returned home. I'm so glad that Snail House is in such good hands. It was a joy to play music there, much of it in remembrance to my grandfather, John Newell who left Hoonah around 1848-1850.

The piano at our church in Hoonah has such a deep rich tone I just let it speak my musical thoughts. It was like a homecoming just being there. One of my most cherished elders from Hoonah was George Betts. He visited us in Sitka often and Victor Johnson gave me his koog'na to wear at the convention. That was another special moment in my life!

Merry Christmas to you both and Happy New Year.

GRANDSONS
December 1, 1987 at Baranof

A new purpose is in my life. I am a baby-sitter. My grandson, Benny Lee Mancil is with me today. I owed him more time than I gave him in the past. With the little work I have done in the past five years, this boy is the most important thing to happen to me.

Such a happy baby! We practiced Samuri sword routines this afternoon. He found great joy in overt arm movements. We laughed with new abandon! He then showed me his favorite book about Sounds of Animals. He would mimic those animals with growls and snorts and even tweets.

He lets me know when it is time for feeding. So we gather at the watering hole and have our way with cereal, soup and macaroni.

I gave him a whole bottle of blood red juice. He drank it all in one sitting. Later, I was scared when a blood like liquid was dribbling out the sides of his mouth. Fear of hemorrhaging or worse raced through my brain. I call mommy and then noticed his gums were lightly bleeding from his teething ring that he used earlier. Saved. I bought a stroller for Benny today. It beats packing, although packing is not that bad.

The biggest thrill of 1994 was on October 24th when little Shelby Victoria Strand was born in Ogden, Utah! I went to Ogden to help out and was there by October 11th. They were expecting the child to be born on November 3rd but fate had other plans.

While there I got acquainted with the Strand family in detail. Tyler Martin David Strand, my grandson, was two and a half years old and my assignment was to take care of him while the baby was being born. 24th Street #526 has bus stoops on both sides of the street and I was excited that I was perceived as a senior citizen by the bus drivers and I paid only 30 cents to get to town.

It was also my honor to take Tyler away from his mother for the first time on a bus ride. We stayed in town a long time and visited the area parks and playgrounds and had a great time. He was a perfect gentleman and enjoyed the trip. It was the beginning of a beautiful friendship Soon we were going to Weber State University and feeding his favorite "dark-wing-ducks."

Ogden is a clean, fine, Republican, Mormon city. I cruised the Thrift Shops with confidence and frequented the good deal pawn shops. My purchases were small but valuable for my camera repair business inventory.

I also found good computer programs that will soon bolster my business records. I would bus to Salt Lake City several times for, you guessed it, only 30 cents! It was my intent to sell some of my excess camera equipment to cover travel expenses but I found few takers. I would wear a rare camera to town and a few people noticed its value and if I stayed longer I think I could have sold it to a select audience.

MARTIN STRAND SR.
Written by Ben Mancil, Martin's oldest grandson, upon Martin Strand's death.

My grandpa had a large influence on my life. When I was young he was my best friend. He would take me everywhere with him in Sitka, in my stroller which he liked to call my limousine.

Later when I got older one of my earliest memories of my grandpa is when he would come to Anchorage to visit. It was like an adventure. We would ride the bus all over town and visit all kinds of great places like the camera store, computer store, pawn shops and thrift stores. We would go to the park to play Frisbee, ride our bikes on the coastal trail and visit the Senior Center for a game of Pool. We were always active and doing something when he was in town. I loved it.

Later I would visit Sitka in the summer and spend all my time with grandpa. I would go over to his house where he had classical music playing loud enough to hear outside and he would always be working on something like one of his cameras or writing about what happened the day before.

When I arrived he was always happy to see me and so was I. He had a lot to do with my love for electronics. I was always fascinated with all the treasures he had in his house, lots of camera equipment, computer equipment, recording equipment and musical instruments.

He loved explaining to me how things worked, leaving out no detail. While I was visiting in Sitka grandpa and I did not waste any time, for every day was an adventure. He had a spare bike for me and we would go everywhere. We would go fishing for dollies at Indian River for hours and afterwards we would go to the park and play Frisbee for hours. I had so much fun as a child in Sitka with my grandpa that I would return every summer.

When I got old enough to go, I would go to fish camp with him. It was a lot of fun and he taught me a lot, like how to set up a tent, sharpen a knife, start a fire and how to clean a fish, sight in a gun and how to properly handle fire arms. I loved every moment I spent with him and I will miss him very much. I wouldn't be the person I am today without him and I am proud to be his grandson. He has done so much for me during my childhood, including being my best friend. I could not have asked for a better grandfather. I love you grandpa.

THE DREAMS OF THE ALASKA NATIVE

Since the millennia of years gone by since we first gathered here
We *first citizens* watched our children grow into a growing world.
Aunts and uncles taught them how to survive under difficult conditions,
Our elders called, gave words of caution and wisdom to the young.
Our focus was always looking to the future with hope.

We had successful relationships with different tribes along the coast.
We often learned to sing their songs and shared their dances.
Part of our traveling currency was to entertain along the way.
In this trading lifestyle we were exposed to some of the finest artwork.
We gladly traded what we had for goods of other Tribes.

Our women wore gold and silver bracelets from the Haidas,
Fine expensive goat wool woven blankets custom designed for us.
We commissioned the opposite clan to make our regalia.
Respect among each other was the order of the day.
We shared the beauty and offerings of Nature.

Well intentioned missionaries came to our shores
And some of us sang along in their song.
We marveled at their talking leaves with strange bird scratches.
That I imagined was the Tlingit's reaction to written pages.
Our Founders wanted us to move into the modern world.

We had to deal with injustice for a long time.
Our grandfathers said, "They will come like a tidal wave.
There is nothing you could do to stop them.
You must learn their language and speak for us later."*
So the young took up the challenge and brought us to today.

Tonight we ask for your help in moving us forward.
We need to call on your fair-mindedness and generosity
To make a better school system for all.
Give us and our children the thirst for excellence our Founders
wanted.
You'll find our doors open and receptive.

* (*Quote: Elder Paul Jackson statement about grandfathers*)

KAASDA HEENI YAAKW CARE TAKERS

The Southeast Alaska Indian Cultural Center passes the care taking
To the Kadushakx, i yis (Canoe Group) with good will to all.
This is an important ceremony for all Sitka witnessing citizens.
The beauty of this moment will live on into the future.
The spirit of the Kaasda Heeni Yaakw (canoe) is now protected.

We step into new cultural waters and lift the canoe out together.
We hope it will serve many special moments yet to come.
Our spiritual footprint of this ceremony would please the ancients.
Our connection to them remains steadfast and close.
The paddles carry the blessing of the community to the Canoe
Group.

*The Southeast Alaska Indian Cultural center transferred maintenance of
the ceremonial canoe (which is called Kaasda Heeni Yaakw) to the Canoe
Group (Kadushakx i yis)*

The ceremony was similar to the dedication of the canoe when it
was finished. The Canoe group took over the maintenance and care
of the canoe from that date forward. There were speeches and canoe
paddles presented from many different organizations. Those who
attended the original canoe dedication and members of the community
were encouraged to attend this important event on May 20th at 4 P.M.
and it was followed by a dinner.

Our depth of pride still matters to us today, especially today.
The Kadushakx, i yis (Canoe Group) is a group of caring citizens.
Their sense of commitment is a strong step forward.
Many of them took part in the canoe idea from the beginning.
They represent all walks of Sitka life intent on responsibility.

The problems of care-taking in ancient days are with us today.
Serious is the word for the ongoing work with the canoe.
The canoe meant years of fruitful service to the Tribe.
Bearing travelers to distant points and bringing fame home
Required skillful maintenance to keep the canoe in readiness.

The water, friend and also enemy, with beauty and danger.
Centuries of boat wisdom gathered by the ancient ones
Brought us forward where we are now on this day.
We gather in respect and admiration for this gift of travel.
We lift our paddles with expectation of the journey.

CALL TO WORSHIP

Grandfather! Hear my cry for wisdom in a troubled world.
Give me a glimpse of the beautiful life as you've seen it.
Show me the way to the new, the renewed life as you've seen it.
Let me live in peace with our neighbors everywhere.

We want the wisdom of John Newell of Snail House.
We want the dedication of Andrew Wannamaker.
We want the steadfastness of Jessie Price
Send us the Hounds of Heaven of Hendrick Van Dyke.
Give us the teaching power of Gladys Whitmore.

Build the strength of our Native way stronger than before.
Lift our hearts as the mountain mists gather around us today.
Ride the waves of the sea and the winds of change.
Live to serve and share that we have known from you.
This is our cry and hope for a better life.

NEVER A LAST DAY

We turned a new page, a new life to bring forward.
After our fears and dreams collided in a trying year.
The Tribe gathered here today is strong and full of hope.
Survival with compassion has drawn us together.
Our children are beginning to understand our ways.

My tears of joy at the young dancers performance was uplifting.
Thankful hearts united in the moment of praise.
Our beautiful lifestyle is threatened occasionally.
We have the tools to fight for justice and eventually peace.
Our Elders speak to us from beyond by their lives.

The smoke slowly rises from the smoke house.
Delectable aroma fills the air with tastes familiar to us all.
The late run coho are running and I gaff one in the stream.
We bring them to grandma Elsie who is joyous at the sight.
Grandpa Ralph takes the eggs to prepare caviar.

Grand Camp meant so much to Ralph and Elsie.
I am beginning to understand the depth of devotion to our people.
I saw it only yesterday on the convention floor so sensitive.
This is the life that was meant to be.
This is our land and our life

My relatives are so vast in numbers and quality.
They have always made me feel like true royalty.
Loving extensions forever reaching out in encouragement.
This is what I remember of my many Elders.
Lifting my spirit without complaint to new heights.

Tonight I reach out and share the best of my life.
Not to be forgotten are those here now.
The candle lights their loving faces.

OUR JOURNEY

This was written for the Archive department of Sitka Tribes of Alaska. I am a volunteer in this project and took a trip to Oklahoma in October of 2007

There was poetry in the way they moved full of purpose.
Their lifestyle was poetic in their thinking and their walking.
I now could see the artistry and oratory in their stories.
It was my wish that I could have recorded their voices.
My Tlingit grandparents are shining memories in my life.

All we have is somewhat crude audio recording of the past.
Some recorded at the slowest speed to stretch out the time.
At that speed the quality was poor at best for music and speech.
But it was a record of the times wanting to reach to the future.
Ancient Native dance and oratory recorded for our time.

It was not part of my world and I could have been a help.
I was building a life of my own and did not look ahead.
The older ones were getting older and leaving the scene.
How I lament the opportunities missed in recording them.
I look to these reel-to reel tapes to do some good for us.

Not understanding the language, I feel the rhythm and meter.
I feel the poetry of those recorded moments bringing a life.
I have pictures of those Elders that paved the way for us.
50 years and more are visually recorded with my camera.
My negatives still have a sharpness and brilliant quality.

Moving from one old format into the new is our task.

How long will these recordings last in the new medium?
When will the equipment become obsolete and die away?
Our future generations are depending on us to save them.
Do I have enough time to make a difference?

We are starting out on a soul searching journey soon.
Looking for the right answers to preserve what we have.
We seek some wisdom of other experts to reveal the truth.
We will lift up our lives with our own strength.
There are valuable moments to be recorded in our journey.

Am I ready to reach out for the help I desperately need?
I want to be responsible for bringing back something of value.
This is not a passing commitment and then moving on.
I will be called on to follow through with good planning.

OUR SPIRITED LIFE
This may be one of my most important jobs of my life

Lifting my spirits to new heights for my people.
The new Kaagwaantaan warrior fights now in kind and caring ways.
Aged faces crack with joyous smiles here including my own.
Happiness looms high in our lives on the horizon.
The familiar becomes in itself the new reality.

The meeting of our minds in this gathering surrounds us.
I feel the greatness of the spirits that have been released.
My Hoonah grandfather's clan leans forward in wisdom.
My grandmother's Kilisnoo people wrap me in warmth.
The building vibrates with energy my blood has known.

Is it any wonder that I should confront the past on my 70th year?
My heart beams a broad smile just for being here.
There is a deep feeling that something good is happening.
It is like I have lived only for these precious moments.
The free spirited birds hover over the sea beneath my window.

Our prayer maiden Linda spoke to us with conviction.
An ancient Haida prayer lingers long and deep into my mind.
The ages seemed to melt away at the simplicity of the poem.
"We will lift our lives with our own strength" she said.
This is what I will carry home caringly to my people.

Into the serious business of today started and stayed with us.
Our highest priority is the way we regard each other.
Our reasons for being here reaches a new understanding.
Insistent voices speak of Tribal wisdom to persuade us.
The things we learned here are part of our journey.

I am challenged to one avenue of thought by our Elders.
Stretching the new depth of my thinking is ever changing.
They speak to me with the smoothness of their life experience.
Their words are stored in the heart to be released later.
Traveling on their same page is part of the excitement.

A NEW HOPE FOR THE YOUNG

With some ancient tools the People carved away on a blessed tree.
A dream slowly becoming reality one day building upon the next.
Suddenly there it was on a sunlit day before us waiting. From the
designers to occasional Enthusiastic contributors were here.
Tribal witnesses full of purpose and hope gathered around.

In the full blossoming of Spring they lifted high the totem.
A willing crowd was up to the task of the long trek.
Lead by the dehydration mobile they slowly moved forward.
They passed the long-gone homes of Bailey and Wells.
Passing the "Cottages" only garage of Louis Shotridge.

Moving on beyond the Daisy "Daniels" Jones house on a rock.
Kelly Street with the Newell, Young, Anderson, and Jacob homes.
Past the "herring eggs drying tree" in brilliant sun they came.
Next the "old Manse" tips its hat as we go by, surrounded by trees.
Then the old Sage building where many learned boat building.

Nearing the flume where I gaffed reddened coho of huge size.
The Native church looks like a library now where the 1965 march
began.
Marching for civil rights, townspeople marched with SJS.
Today we march with just as much meaning as then.
Hold high the lives of our youth in an ever changing world.

What was the dramatic curve of the Crescent we march through.
My sister, Sofia, and I hand in hand walked to school on this beach.
In the winter high tides, the waves splashed high over the breakwater.
We waited in the shadow of the Episcopal church till the wind went
down.
The Charlotte and Glen Morgan small house was in white and green.

The totem was carried past the house of tour guide Charlie Haley.
His sister was a famous harp musician of great ability.
Inspector Hallum guides with a smile, cars along the way.
A lot of thought was carried out for the safest of travel.
Inter-generational people lift with confidence the spirit of the tree.
The parade stops in front of my first school on Lincoln street.
I remember teacher Mrs. Rowe. In second grade here.

The Elders listen to the beating drum in future hope for the young.
The emotion of the moment runs high in this growing crowd.
They sing songs our blood has known for generations.
Today we visited bygone days of Tribal splendor and vanished glory of
fighting times.

RURAL DETERMINATION

This is testimony at a hearing about our customary and traditional lifestyle.
I stood up with my peers in this public talk. September 24, 2006.

Our lifestyle is deeply threatened once again in Sitka.
The exciting tastes of our culture came to me early.
One of many fish camps in Nakawasina Bay thrived.
My 8th and 9th year {1943-1944} was the beginning.
We could hardly sleep for the roar of fish jumping.

The smoke house, filled to the rafters with salmon.
A hanging deer being smoked in a dark corner.
Seal heart and liver with potatoes for supper.
Blueberry and salmon berry cups of delight.
I dragged a gaffed, confused humpy to Grandma.

Later, my brother John and I would hunt for deer.
He knew how to hunt, fish and trap splendidly.
My first boat was used constantly throughout the seasons.
Ducks and geese in time for Thanksgiving dinner.
The fall and winter clam tides helped our needs.
We enjoy keeping Sitka rural as my ancestors enjoyed.
Our tribal connections to the land and sea are strong.
We share our traditional and cultural resources
With our extended tribal families in this area.
It is a beautiful lifestyle of caring my blood has known.

In my 71st year I still receive blessings of land and sea.
Hunters and fishers make sure we are well fed.
Our Swan Lake Senior center cooks our cultural food.
I am fishing jack salmon and deer hunting this season.
Although my involvement is an ancient echo I am glad.

I rise in praise of a rural Sitka because it is our nature.
It would be a disappointment to lose this quality of life.
Utilizing our fish and wildlife privileges would be a great loss.
I reach out in hope for continued blessings from land and sea.
Please use these comments in the good spirit given.

THE JOURNEY

This was written after midnight heading to Hoonah. It was so dark all I could see was the blinking red and green lights of the buoys. I always have dreamed of kayaking to Hoonah and this is the result of my dream. Into the fading night we rode the moving ferry.

The gentle sea swells were hardly noticed in our glide.
Sitka left behind, lights fading rapidly now facing the blackness.
Hearts warm with expectation we gladly looked ahead.
Focusing our thoughts on our mission was our real goal.

The time dripped slowly as the mists struck our window.
The eight second blinked green to the starboard.
The menacing red blinked danger to the other side.
Moving to an ever deep sleep, rest overtook us.
Dreams of the good ahead we planned for our people.

The canoe pulled ahead with the strength of ten men.
Dripping water the only sound as the paddles lifted.
Our resting spot for the night only ten miles away.
Moonlight on the shimmering wind--swept sea.
Lifting the canoe high up the beach we then rested.

October morning heavy with gray dew droplets everywhere.
The paddles idle under the canoe as breakfast was made.
A faint glimmer of sun lifts over the mountains.
We speak softly to each other with deep respect.
Our leader motions his arm to the waiting sea.

We think kindly of the people of Hoonah days ahead.
Our gifts are carefully boxed in the hold for the right time.
Our hunters got three deer and a seal at our last stop.
Their hunting skill is considerable and we are thankful.
Eagles are successful fishing all around us.

A short distance away from Hoonah we pull out and rest.
It is time to prepare for our entrance to the village.
We drum around the final bend and they hear us coming.
Their drum and welcoming songs fill the air.
We have arrived at the best part of our journey.

NOVEMBER MOMENT

Shadows of my past visit me in the graying of the afternoon.
Shallow thoughts race through my mind as if they have a place.
Kaagwaantaan of the warrior class brings military tasks.
The Eagle Nest House weighs heavily, deep into my own soul.
I hear the somber past death voice of my Koohuk grandfather.
Lovingly he speaks urging me to gather closer to my People.

Dwee is there looking at me from the kitchen and wondering.
Her hopes for my life are insistent that I follow their way.
Amid the hot smoked salmon stew that fills my life I listen.
The back door opens as they bring in the recently butchered seal.
I am directed to go to the smoke house to check the fire embers.

Tlingit is spoken in musical and poetic ways working into my mind.
There is deep respect I feel as they go over the details of the day.
Kaagwaantaan uncles come in from the skinning shed to be filled.
There are Ravens nearby knowing that the Thanksgiving feast is near.
My sister and I listen from the stairs to the Tribal activity going on.
Not understanding the words but we realize the caring meaning of them.
The stories go on into the night, rich with translations that we get to know.
The smiles, the gestures, the body language come together for us.
Bilingual expressions of where we are today float throughout the room.
Thoughts of ANB and ANS reach to a much higher place in that evening.

Today I grieve that my life was not made more full learning the language.
I see the improvements it made in my own children's learning program.
It gave them something more than monetary rewards, it gave them a soul.
Perhaps, the depth of their learning was not deep enough.
But the fruits of the experience into language and dance speak volumes.

I ponder whether I should go to the language meeting this afternoon.
What could I contribute to the ongoing quest to revive the language?
The few words and phrases I know are shrouded in insignificance.
I get caught up in the emotion of the music, dance and emotion.
It is an ancient longing my blood has known long before childhood.

SITKA NATIVE EDUCATION PROGRAM TESTIMONY

Testimony of Marcia and Martin Strand March 1, 2004 at the ANB Hall

Our Founders and Elders of ANB and ANS pushed high the priority of a good education from the beginning. Their struggle has been a long and hard one with some success along the way. We have worked through the School District over the years to give our children a chance for a better life.

We applaud the success of the Sitka Native Education Program in several fronts: regionally, local and personal. Marcia and I thank the program every day for our children Sara, Martina, and Martin Jr. Learning Indian culture when our grandparents were no longer with us, each one has been with SNEP for ten years. The powerful Native role models they met with over the years taught them respect for our Culture in its inner beauty in art and dance. The thousands of dollars well spent on our family alone leaves us obligated to see that the program continues into the future.

We understand that the flow of money comes from Federal dollars directly to the School District. The SNEP program was created by local Indian people to use these dollars to immerse the children in every way into the Native culture. Marcia and I were on hand from the inception of SNEP, serving as members of the Parent Committee.

The students gather at the ANB Hall after school in a user--friendly atmosphere. The pictures on the walls show where we've been as first citizens, culturally rich and growing. An ideal setting for teaching dance, art, and regalia making. Things our Founders would love to know that are carried on beyond their lives. We sincerely hope that the program can continue at its present location, teaching and holding the Cultural banner high.

We need continuing education training for our SNEP director and teachers.
Under Isabella Brady and the Parent Committee this has been going on. Historically nationwide there have been abuses in the use of IEA monies. Abuses of travel funds and poorly informed parents and Indian community. We need our SNEP director to be active in all the planning and vision decisions that are to be made. Please keep the funding for this most valuable program.

Sincerely,

SITKA NATIVE EDUCATION
PROGRAM
A REMEMBRANCE

SNEP has had a significant impact in the lives of our children since its inception. In the beginning it was such a distant dream that we could have a rich cultural program. The earliest vision of our Founders was to give our children the best of our culture in a deep education context. We Strands praise the program for giving our children powerful self--esteem and wanting to be excellent in everything they do. The gift of teamwork in language and dance gave them a running start in their lives.

Isabella Brady gathered the finest teachers of the time to put together a winning program funded with grants and other sources. Willing Elders rallied around the program, imparting their valuable time and wisdom to assure success. Sara, Martina and Martin Jr. would come home bubbling with enthusiasm for language, art and dance. These were the happy days, unfolding into weeks, months and then years. They each put in ten years of experience in the SNEP program.

Marcia and I gladly played a part in some of the beginning of the program "Food The Native Way!" Elders Sara and Ed James, Marietta Williams, Ida Peters, George Anderson and others took an active part in willingly helping that vision to come to reality. Roby and John Littlefield's Dog Point fish camp was an idea setting for learning. In 1984 I shot a 150 pound seal in Nakawisina Sound and brought it to the hall and Sara James demonstrated the proper way of dressing it so none of it was wasted.
There were lots of hands-on opportunities to clam dig, smoke salmon, and gather herring eggs. Living off the land and sea was

always a component of the teaching. It was from Marietta Williams I first heard the phrase, "when the tide goes out the table is set."

It was my personal honor to photograph much of the program over the years. It was an additional joy in my life to photograph my children in their dance regalia at the ANB hall for special events. I remember the fire in the eyes of Charlie Joseph as he taught his "Angels" to sing and dance. They were motivated by the caring ways he expressed his great wisdom. His daughter, Ethel, carried on the tradition and now his granddaughter, Laura, is doing a good job running the program today.

There are so many exciting components of the SNEP program and we are glad to keep them running. We will always come forward to help in any way we can when the need arrives. It has been a program tried and true and full of success. We are so full of thanks in a personal way for what it has done for our family over the years. It is the source of much happiness to our Elders at every performance and every victory.

WONDROUS LIFE STYLE

{Testimony to a wondrous lifestyle from the Strands, 5th of May, 2000}

We gather in praise of the original people that sparked the
Sitka Native Education Program to its cultural journey.
Our esteemed Elder, Charlie Joseph, a man with a vision,
Gave breath to the mission statement of the program.
He is central to the life of our children as we see them today.

My children's voyage into this exciting lifestyle is not diminished by
time.
They would all want to be here today to share this important event.
Their total involvement spanned 28 years of intense learning and fun
times.
Preparation to speak and dance with confidence were taught.
Elder respect and caring for others is a special lesson to them.

Sara Joy, Martina Rae and Martin Junior remember their friends.
Over the years they have kept contact with their special ones.
Their eyes sparkle approvingly as we bring them news of SNEP.
I remember the joy of all the trips they made outside of town.
We realize the broadening, sharing and knowledge of other cultures.

Our family is full of thanks for what we could not do alone.
The gathering of wisdom behind such a brilliant program.
The legions of Elders leading the way into the future.
We grieve the loss of those valued ones along the way.
We celebrate the contribution their lives have made on us.

The joy of seeing the young making their way forward is happiness.
Supported lovingly along the way is the support staff.
Cultural values are a strong part of this important vision.

The spiritual ways of the Ancients, the Founders are here.
We bask in deep pride just to be here today as witnesses.

Our mission is to advocate and support this worthwhile effort.
We hope the program will not be threatened in the future.
We gather our positive feelings and dreams for success.
This is something important for the Children's esteem building.
We hope to help your efforts to go forward confidently.

KAYAKER

The Kaagwaantaan kayaker takes to the sea tomorrow.
Just before dawn his lone figure makes its way down the dock.
A double kayak waits with a small paddle at the ready.
He is no stranger to this type to travel.
It is a silent and effective way to hunt.

The slow, deliberate travel makes for a reasoned hunt.
He passes the point where twenty years ago we caught a swimmer.
He remembers the Northern stormy winter winds that come up suddenly.
The long successful shot with 264 rifle on the flats.
The surprise of 100 geese rising around a corner of the bay.

It's Halloween, in other times the snow suddenly falls.
Frozen nights and sometimes rain, snow, and sudden sunshine.
Swimming deer move from island to island perhaps, I'll see one today.
Binoculars carefully adjusted are by my side waiting.
My 223 rifle is there with full metal jackets of 55 grains.

The water is calm at 5:45 as the craft is launched.
A few deft strokes and I'm on my way to the North.
I start a consistent rhythm and aim for the first point.
Scooter ducks flee as I approach them and they are airborne.
Paranoid mallards fly straight up in fear since the season's open.

A slight ripple of waves moved by a light wind.
Water from the paddles drips down my arms.
A light fog hangs low on the mountain sides.
Images flash on my mind where I got them before.
The scene is set for some action and I look deeper ahead.

I stop near a small river and bring the binoculars into play.
300 yards to the east I think I see a deer and paddle there.
On closer observation the stump never seems to move.

A rough legged hawk chases a greater yellowlegs near the trees.
Twelve Canadian honkers take off up the bay coming my way .
I see their black backs but their white breasts disappear when they turn.

Dog salmon creek shows green winged teal, pintails and mallard.
A greater blue heron squawks a warning and flies away.
Coho jumping nearby in bright silver recall my youth at camp.
We smoked salmon in the Fall in this bay with grandparents.
The boat "Smiles" was our headquarters at Nawkasina Bay.

Dolly Varden trout splash beneath the kayak at the river.
They run a strong ten pounds and I'm tempted to fish for them.
We used to catch 50 here and take them to the smoke house.
Grandpa Ralph made me my first gaff from a spruce sapling.
At age eight I caught disoriented humpies on the waters edge.

Traveling so silently I come upon a deer feeding quietly.
It was down at the rifles bark and I went ashore.
Quickly dressing it I started back to the cabin for butchering.
The camp was glad once again to have food for the smoke house.
A dinner of heart and liver was enjoyed by all.
The hot tea burns my cold lips as I take a break.
It feels so good to be alive in such a setting.

Dog Point fish camp

CHAPTER 2 DOG POINT FISH CAMP

DOG POINT FISH CAMP

Things to take: Survival Kit
knives and sharpeners
check matches
leather and cord
Frisbees
Trout Fishing equipment
Binoculars
computer paper

Reloading supplies
223 dies
6.5x55 dies
223 brass
6.5x55 brass
small rifle primers
large rifle primers
Priming tools (large & small)
Case mouth reamer
case lube & pad
loading tool & shell holders
Powder measure & clamp
Powder scale
Powder W630 & 4831

223 & 6.5 bullets
Micrometer
Case trimmer & collets for
223 & 6.5
Lee Loader primer punch
Manual for loads (Speer)
22 Ruger & bullets
Targets & round labels
Stapler (or one in camp)
Cleaning rods for guns & clean
those guns in advance
Lube for gun actions
Gun bluing kits & sandpaper
Gun shooting rest
Proper screw drivers
Hex wrenches
Boots and shoes
Socks & briefs
hankies & tee shirts
Pants and shirts
Rain gear
My writing about camp life
Pictures of camp etc.
"Things to do" Sharpen camp knives
Clam shell competitions
Make whistles
Gun safety course
Rifle range sessions
Range length 50 & 100 yards
Make target area
Trout fishing in Nakawisina
Teach fire starting
Computer paper airplanes
Cut wood for Smokehouse and
Cabin & sauna
Get into the water
Recite poetry

Martin R. Strand, Sr.

Students interview Elders
Seal hunting
Make Slingshots (rubber band)
Frisbee gold and distance throw.
Take some music tapes
Perhaps, CDs music appreciation
Tell hunting & fishing stories
Boating safety
Bird watching course
Great Elders I have known
My life in early Sitka
How I became a photographer
My interest in music
Broadcasting experience.

THE DOG POINT PAPERS

My ancient ritual means something today.
Tribal uncles would bark the orders of the day.
Bringing the youth to awareness of nature by instruction.
Hunting and fishing skills also would be taught
Parents watching from a loving distance rejoice.

I'm standing knee deep in the sea and loving it.
The sea opens its arms as a friend and does not threaten.
The men of Dog Point rejoice among themselves for half an hour.
The strengthening ritual is completed by diving under the water.
We walk refreshed to the warmth of the sauna.

Our plan is to discuss, motivate, urge, persuade, then hope.
As aunties, uncles, and teachers we strive to share.
The lesson plan is lifestyle past, present and future.
Our past is a colorful canvas of famous lives that glisten.
Our animal designs speak of our respect for nature.

I remember my own joy of harvest time at Nakawasina Bay.
The intense energy of getting salmon for the smoke house.
The skill of the women in preparing the dry fish.
The afternoon salmon berry pickers would return with gallons.
Fish heads and tails, along with backbones for a royal supper.

Opening the good of the past is the Dog Point Fish Camp.
Old reflections of my early camp life quicken at our camp.
Today we work with deer, seal, sea otter and fish.
Newly sharpened knives silently fillet, slice and parry.
Sizzling on the kitchen stove a surprise supper cooks.

We're busy opening windows for the youth.

How fond of wood cutting they are.
Watchful elder eyes warn of axe danger.
Helping with food preparation is a high priority.

I will never regret this adventure I took risks.
Many of them in outlook, writing or design
My shirt buttons would burst in pride.
Seeing the positive things the youth are doing here.
Good listeners, keen eyes and bright minds.

All too soon the day ends and time for dreaming begins.
Enveloping night is welcomed like a warm friend.
Tree tops fade and the evening star winks at us.
Lazy clouds to the west reflect on the shimmering sea.
A rich feeling of accomplishment draws us to deep sleep.

Preparing salmon for smoking

FRIDAY FRIGHT NIGHT

Our day had its ups and downs.
Our rifle club carried on in the afternoon.
The tide was rapidly rising as we started shooting.
Jordan Gray and Andrew Rezek shot scores of 17 which forced a
shootout.
It looked like they had 8 points on the second try.
But on closer examination Jordan's shot cut the 9 ring.
What a finish. This puts Jordan's aggregate score up to first hunter.
He joins a long line of hunters in his family.

King salmon heads, salsa, rice and herring eggs for lunch.
Fresh white king salmon, corn, rice and pickled blueberries at night.
Betty and 5 students were in town for Science lab to return at 8:30
Fifteen minutes after their estimated departure I saw FOG.
It was rapidly coming toward us down the straights.
I alerted Roby who immediately recognized the danger.
She and Stephan took the boat to search for Betty's boat
They came back for a compass as visibility was rapidly dropping.
Out they go on the search as night and fog was falling.

Roby's boat came back when they realized they couldn't read the
compass.
They wanted to have someone aboard that could use the compass.
At this time I talked them into making a phone call to Sitka.
While we were getting ready to call, Betty phoned us saying all's well.
They went up Katlean Bay when the fog started lowering.
Fortunately, they got back to Sitka with nearly empty gas cans.
Dog Pont had no way of knowing they were lost and we prepared for
searching.
We followed survival search techniques recognizing the problem.
We were thinking of signal systems so the missing boat could see us.

The best idea was to light up the scow and fire guns once in a while. To compound the problem Roby's cell phone battery konked out. She could hear them but they couldn't hear us. Meanwhile, another crisis arose.
Two boys imagined a bear near their tent and ran to the cabin. It took Grandma Lydia and Travis Cole quite a while to calm them down.
Finally, Roby gave them an option to stay in their tents or a cabin. They chose their tent.

Doing chores

RADIANT MORNINGS & STILL NIGHTS

I'm a salesman.
My smile has a lot of mileage on it.
Sometimes sincere other times not.
I'm as good as I want to be.

Wanting to do things that are worthwhile
I stumble often on my own feet.
I have visions of where I ought to be.
Places good I should show up.

One of those places is the Dog Point Fish Camp.
Here we buy time in the lives of youth.
This is our mission to bring them to the future.
Also, to enjoy our rich, cultural past.

It is the most dangerous and deadly game.
Giving youth strong reasons to go on.
Everything we do means something to them.
Our open book lives sometimes betray us.

But we must do the best we can with what we've got.
With lessons in Tlingit we carry the flame.
Preparing our traditional food we look to tomorrow.
We retreat to the silence of the nourishing sleep.

While in my bed I have visions of the past.
What grandparents might have thought of me.
If they could see my reflection today.
Weighed in the balance and found wanting?

I shot at two seal and missed.
I handed my gun to Steve and he connected.
Young eyes and body are superior.
Gladly I shared my equipment for that moment.

Four Killer Whales preceded our rescue.
We briefly followed them after the boat was going.
Inspiration from nature always helps in hope.
We followed the steps to our survival.

Watching the young girls prepare skins for drums
On a sunny Wednesday before I left camp
Gave me a powerful feeling of triumph.
They are doing what the ancients would have done.

The depth of beauty of the camp life is deep.
Nature winking at us around every corner.
A curious bear checks out the camp that night
The dogs bark loudly and the bear is gone.

Just before dawn I see bats coming home over the trees.
You can tell them at great distances with butterfly flight.
My picture window reveals a minus tide way out.
My mind searches for a clam shovel that isn't there.

Our tribe is made up of hunters and fishers.
It is our nature to gather fish and game.
We live by what the seasons give us.
Gladly we harvest what nature offers.

I wondered where these young lives were going.
I wrote a story about each one in fantasy lives.
It was great fun to make up positive lifestyles
For each one and myself.

Poetic ideas come easily in the night and morning.
Sometimes I got up and wrote some fleeting idea.
It was worth it to be in this creative place.
I feel I'm in the right place at the right time.

Roby and John full of hope and expectation
Guide the thoughts and action daily.
It is worthwhile just to be a small part of it.
The elders also sparkle giving the young a future.

Seeing the work of the community come together
Is a wonder to behold.
We wait for another Radiant Morning as we
Dream another Still night.

AUGUST SIXTH SENSE

My sleep was so deep I drowned in restfulness.
The thrilling part of Dog Point nights is having no lights.
At 2 A.M. I had to consider how to get downstairs in the dark.
My matches are in my survival kid, but wait! I have an
Ancient waterproof match container in my pants pocket.

I strike a match and it fizzles then another catches on
And briefly brightens the room. I could have cursed the
Darkness but I lit the match like the old Chinese proverb.
It was so dark and serene. I could hear myself think.
How many places in the world could make that statement?

Candles were a part of my youth at our fish camp.
"Bring out the candles, grandson," grandpa Young would say.
And if I was a good boy I could light one or two.
Small pleasures were mine from time to time at the smoke house.
I would look for humpies along the shore with my gaff.

Sarah, Lucy and Jordan picked ninety percent of the blueberries
For our breakfast this morning.
What a treat with syrup and melting butter.
Campfire baked salmon heads by campfire last night.
The flavor was inspiring.

I will never regret this adventure I took with risks
Many of them in outlook, writing or design.
My shirt buttons again bursting with pride
Seeing the positive things the youth are doing here.
Good listeners, keen eyes and bright minds.

All too soon the day ends and time for dreaming begins.
Enveloping night is welcomed like a warm friend.
The tree tops fade and the even star winks again.
Lazy clouds to the west reflect on the simmering sea.
A rich feeling of accomplishment draws us to deep sleep.

CAMP LIFE

Ten king salmon from the Hatchery were well appreciated.
We had fish head stew to the delight of all.
The rest of the fish were cut in strips for a partial smoke.
They would be put in jars for eating later.
The sweet alder smoke drifted over the camp.

Echoes of my boyhood were everywhere in my mind.
This was not unlike the Nakawsina camp in the 1940s.
The same serene scene now interrupted by modern boats passing by.
Or a Coast Guard helicopter out on call up the straits.
A lonely seal comes near the camp borders.

We are here to give vision to what might be.
We live to pass on the lessons we have learned.
To, hopefully, eager students that have a future.
The heads of the Elders nod approvingly as they see progress.
The students' eyes brighten as we all pull forward.

Lisa sang as she cleaned the Dog Point Hilton when I arrived.
There were colorful, dusty old bottles inside the window.
She took them outside put them on a pillar and let the rain wash
them.
They were so beautifully arranged I photographed them.
It was my most significant photograph of the year 2000.

It many ways we depend on each other in camp.
It is a team effort for the young and old the way we work.
New hands cut the fish for the smoke house.
The ancients spin some wisdom for us to hear.
As we learn about each other we become closer.

There is a new fire pit in Uncle John's kitchen.
King salmon wrapped in cabbages leaves are placed around the fire.
A little less than an hour they are ready for supper.
And what a meal along with fried goose tongue salad.
The remains were used for king salmon bagels in the morning.

The work around camp is started but more needs to be done.
We bask in the water then warm up in the sauna.
The thought of leaving this sacred ground even briefly is sad.
What the centuries have given to the Littlefields is waiting for us.
We have been culturally refreshed for the time being.

EMBRACE THE FLOWER FROM THE HEART
June 17, 2004

Facing the stiff wind from the South my kayak bobs like a cork.
It's 8:30 P.M., as I push off for Dog Point and the light begins to fade.
I remember the many times I made this fulfilling voyage in the past.
This time is much more special because Hawaiians await.
New found friends bring a special flavor to my life.

We share our cultures with such a freedom of movement.
Our dances take on historic proportions as they are drummed.
People of the sea unite surrounded by our way of life.
Depending on the Mother Sea giving life to our living.
The good my grandparents gave me reflects strongly today.

Sharing moments of joy and grief in memorable ways
We recall our Elders words of strength and wisdom.
The Forest Service bending a listening ear of help
Joins us in loving care of the land and sea.
Our conversation on a two way street toward understanding.

I see the children on an upward slope toward adulthood.
A few short years they will be making their mark on society
It looks like a good mark from where I stand hopefully.
We walk together for a short while sharing our dream.
I spoke my heart many times with the help of other poets.

We worked hard and played hard for several days.
Balanced thinking in looking at each other's culture.
The good of each prevailed in this loving setting by the sea.
Littlefields surrendered their time and talents and land.
We stand here and look at them in pure worship

Synthesizer in service

WE GO TO DOG POINT FISH CAMP
July 31, 2006

In June, July and August we go to Dog Point Fish Camp where I teach .

In June I took part in the Dog Point Fish Camp. 15 students from 6 to 14 made up the camp in addition to the instructors. I taught gun safety and put on a camp wide competition to determine who would be our seal hunter. Young Tony appeared to be the most advanced in shooting skills. On our hunt we were in range of two seals but the bouncing sea was restless and we did not shoot. My health was quite good at camp.

The boys and girls ask questions about the ammunition I'm loading up today. My mind again feeling young answers. Such an interest in learning inspires me. The business of camp increases hourly. The satisfaction of teaching is strong.

I'm getting used to the youthful idea of "Let's get it done now!" Most of my life has been, "we'll finish this tomorrow." I'm beginning to see the youthful approach more and more each day. These are some of the benefits of Dog Point.
The tide with a life of its own races in and out with such speed I gasp in amazement. Is time moving so fast when you enjoy it most! 1 king salmon, 2 coho and 3 dog salmon are caught in the camp gill net yesterday. So many lives pulling together at once in an uncommon desire to succeed. I've known the mission of this camp for a very long and deeply rewarding time. The Littlefield's dream now is so real. It is a village like no other, an atmosphere found in no other place.
Just before the July camp I was working on my bike. I have picked it up and turned it over many times in the past. But this time I sprained my back. Dr. Blake inspected me along with X-rays and gave me a prescription to use in addition to Tylenol. I thought it wise to stay

away from Fish Camp this time. I healed slowly and today hardly notice the problem except when sitting for long periods.

Since I saw you last time I had an eye test. I see slightly double images of birds 200 yards and over. Another thing I noticed when I see people across the street it seems they have two eye brows. One on top of the other.

I mentioned numbness in my small toes. I think it is more stiff skin than numbness. The ointment you gave me seems to help and I put it on after a bath.

Deer hunting seasons begins tomorrow and I plan to take part in several hunts this season. My guns are sighted in and I load my own bullets in my loading press. I plan to fish for trout and jack salmon in Indian River when the time is right. I have not kayaked in a long time. I feel I should work out to get back in shape by taking short trips to the islands. My poetry and musical experience is growing.

SUNDAY WITH MUCH CHARACTER

Written on the camp typewriter

Overcome by heavy sleep I dreamed deeply. Overeating at supper, my stomach upsets. The candle flickers in the night and dies. I dream of huge deer and large bears chasing each other in great fun.

The beautiful silence gives me strength. It has such value at this time of my life.
Why did it take so long to find it? It's much better late than never, There is something to "quiet" signs in libraries.

The boys and girls ask questions about the ammunition I'm loading up today. My mind again feeling young, answers. Such an interest in learning inspires me. The busyness of camp increases hourly. The satisfaction of teaching is strong.

I'm getting used to the youth ful idea of, "Let's get it done now!" Most of my life has been, "Well finish this tomorrow." I'm beginning to see the youthful approach more and more each day. This is one of the benefits of Dog P:oint.
I'm filling my days with fresh memories, the smile of discovery of a learning child. Ancient stories told so well by an Elder. The young girls do research on seal oil.

Long blades of green shore grass swallow, swallow the seaweed strewn shoreline. Light, foggy rain swirls around us. Its splash is less than a memory. I step into the cold sea and am refreshed.
Wading up to my neck the water warms. Remembering a more youthful time I cry. I tipped over on my raft and opened my eyes to an exciting marine life below. Discovery and all it gives are mine.

Now I live for fish camp and all its good. Kingfishers intent on love chase each other. How erratic is their courtship flight. Ancient barked trees with evergreen sparkle. Just being here is the best medicine.

The tide with a life of its own races in and out with such speed I gasp in amazement. Is time moving so fast when you enjoy it most? One king salmon, two cohoe, and three dog salmon are caught in the camp gill net yesterday.
So many lives pulling together at once in an uncommon desire to succeed. I've known the mission of this camp for a very long and deeply rewarding time. The Littlefields' dream now is so real.
It is a village like no other, an atmosphere found in no other place.

LIFE AT THE DOG POINT HILTON
June, 2000

There was mortal combat going on outside my window.
The silence was so deep you could cut it with a knife.
An orderly matrix of webs was the scene of battle.
There was a spider family in full summer operation on their nets.
The afternoon heat alongside the building lifted insects into the web.

The spiders quickly put an end to their prey and carried them away.
I've never seen a spider family working diligently together.
I used to think they were loners and independent but not anymore.
It was a team effort working together during the harvest months.
We work that way with our beach seine during our fishing season.

I had a panoramic view of Dog Point from my upstairs window.
Heavy rain did not dampen our spirits because we are so glad to be
here.
The rain would stop soon and we went about our work.
This trip was to get the camp in shape for the July event.
We will be working with fish, deer, seal and edible plants.

When I came to the cabin Joy Light had scrambled eggs and ham for
us.
What an opening great start for the first day!
This high spirited lady was an inspiration to all of us.
We later learned she was an actress of note and lived a rich full life.
She added a sense of drama to the camp with her stories.

Uncle John Littlefield did not get a chance to come to camp this
time.
His work lately was so demanding on his time.
When here he takes command of the camp with his wisdom.

He and his sons are great outdoors men and love to be here.
Last year he made a deer call out of a dollar bill and called up a bear.

An ever moving stream of activity is Roby Littlefield.
She commands a deep cultural awareness with a strong side of
language.
For her there is no detail too large or small that she can not handle.
When there is pressure at camp activities she is at her best.
She jumps in with the work whatever it might be.

WHEN I MISS DOG POINT FISH CAMP

Looking at my life tonight I see needful areas long gone.
My music listening is suffering greatly.
I whistle fewer songs from the many I have known.
Perhaps eight to ten songs are my current repertoire.
My upper whistle range is compromised by my hearing.

A lifetime of listening to great music is fading.
It was such a joy in the 90's to listen alone.
To let the music speak to me in magical ways.
To mold my thoughts in artistic, creative times.
Now as my mind diminishes in capacity I falter.

It takes longer to identify familiar pieces I have known.
The Sitka Community Band is a help to my music.
I have opened doors to the past with this group.
The technique brings back old musical thoughts.
This would be the key to my late life growth.
To keep alert and active is my goal.

My Casio 670 keyboard brings me new happiness.
Voices I missed with my other keyboard are now there.
All I need to get started with my CD music software is a monitor.
A 256 color monitor will be my next improvement.

I've missed two Dog Point Fish Camp outings this year.
June and July are gone but I have August 18th to begin.
Part of me died just missing those important outings.
I will put my whole self into making the best of it.
There is so much I want to share of my life with others.

Sighting in the rifle

OPPORTUNITY JUST IN TIME
March 25, 2001

Stiff Western wind brought cold, clear skies to Dog Point.
Herring and whales, herring and whales are intent in purpose
Flip and jump to let us know it is their time.
Setting the stage for all this a light snow before the season opens.
The advance team arrives at fish camp to open our minds.

The picturesque setting glistens in the noontime sun.
Centuries old beauty reaches much further than we could see.
Ancestors peek from the shadows, approving our being here.
Their dream became our reality and our lifestyle.
Annie and John Littlefield's land brought us our future.

Caring duties bring us into a glowing afternoon rising tide.
Our light plant needs repair and is lifted dockside.
Near eventide our thoughts turn to the coming hunting days.
Vanessa with charm and skill shoots a two inch group at 100 paces.
The instructor is visibly pleased and full of praise.

The night is cold with warm thoughts at this most special place.
Freezing winds from the Northwest send growing ice blocks to the
bay.
My wall is the sundial familiar to me from the past.
The sun's first rays peek over the hemlock grove to the East.
Two Kingfishers land on the weather-beaten tree across the cove.

The rest of the team arrives before noon with enthusiasm for their mission.
The youth also come, some of them for the very first time.
They take to the Cabin that will be their home for the next few days.
Elders are alive with stories and commentary about past and present.
The Spirit of Dog Point reaches out and binds us once again.

This is the love of my un-lived life so brightly before me.
I will go away from here many times only to return hopeful.
It gives me the sparkle I need to face our uncertain world.
Inspiration shines in every corner and moves rapidly outward.
I am here to share and be shared for those lucky enough to be here.

The youth seem so willing to take part and help where needed.
Something about the Great Outdoors opens doors long dormant.
Fewer distractions are here and there is time to think.
Programs custom coordinated to the youth unfold.
We start on a journey that will make all of us see more clearly.

The sun falls on the coldest night and the heat is small at bedtime.
A light tinkling of ice in the bay increases as the wind thickens.
Stories of long ago connect us to the vision of Camp.
It all happened here where ancient canoes were hauled out.
The Gathering of Canoes stopped here to prepare for potlatch.

We made plans for bringing food back for the April gathering.
Just like the olden days planning began long before the event.
Our mission is to teach and learn respect for each other.
Respect for the land and its creatures is uppermost with us.
Caring, loving, sensitive, and firm are the way of the Tribe.

Our traditional meals are enjoyed by all those here.
Baked salmon, moose meat on rice, and herring roe breakfasts
Give us strength to live and learn the good way.
After meals we are grateful for the youth helping prepare for
tomorrow.
Things around camp soon fall into place and free us to listen.

Our Founder of camp tells us a story about sea lion hunters.
We all listen intently and remember the details.
That's how our oral tradition has carried on in the past.
Our totem poles are our written expression of who we are.
Our oral tradition is kept in the memory of our people.

Herring egg harvest is heavy on our minds.
Branches are cut and made ready to be submerged along the shore.
Indications are the herring will spawn soon.
Reports of some spawning to the south of us.
Branches will be set sometime near low tide.

A party of three hunters finds a window of opportunity for a hunt.
Heavy rain moves in from the west but they continue.
Almost time to turn back they find a large beach with a river.
At the river several seal gather before dark.
Our lady sharpshooter takes one well aimed shot and we have a seal!

Another boat checking herring areas spots an expired sea lion.
We decide to harvest it for its fine pelt and pick it up.
All this activity is opportunity to teach and young hands on
experience.
There are many willing workers and the Elders are also encouraged.
A passing boat brings in fresh crab and it is enjoyed by all.

During the evenings I have an opportunity to write about Camp.
There is so much action I soon have pages done.
I write a little history, some mystery of the past, and with a lot of
hope.
A lot of the feelings are the same over the years but the faces change.
There is too much of my ancestral history here to reflect.

THE DOG POINT DAILY
July, 2004

Deep in the recess of my mind I reach out to Dog Point Fish Camp.
Being no stranger to the magical quality of this place I smile.
Reaching toward the mission of excellence we gather for the work.
The students are here and ready to learn what we have.
Beauty with serenity is what we offer along with cultural lessons.

Another sun lit day I awake early in the quiet of a summer morning.
The birds are already active as they soar in a gentle wind.
Hump backed salmon jump high to see where they are today.
They see the entrance to Nakawsina Bay, the jewel of the harvest.
We know that the smoke house will be active soon.

Young energy emerges everywhere and bounces off the camp.
New minds are opened to a lifestyle that has lived here long ago.
Dog Point history reflects the lives that lived to the fullest.
Canoes were pulled out here to prepare for "potlatch" in Sitka.
Traces of those long--gone still linger in our minds as stories are told.

The food gathering continues, the hunting culture still survives.
The ancient crafts bring out new meaning to those learning.
The songs are learned along with the descriptive movements of the
dance.
The blade skillfully fillets the sockeye in preparation for smoking.
Racks of red flesh glisten in the sun and alder smoke surrounds them.

Kingfishers fly nearby and the flying lady has a red belt on her breast.
A sudden dive and a small fish is taken from the surface of the sea.
A seal is seen working the bay for another mouthful of salmon.
I sip Hudson Bay tea flavored with a dash of sugar as I look outward.
Tim prepares strong coffee that he calls "Mud" and is satisfied.

Tlingit women are here adding their beauty to the spirit of the camp.
My grandson, Benny, now 17 was here when he was 10 years old.
I am proud of the way he helps the camp and he feels good.
Three young ladies are winners in the 22 shootout.
Their scores are 26, 9, and 5 and they shot under quite a bit of
pressure.

Roby and John Littlefield run the camp with authority and
compassion.
The boat is busy daily ferrying people and supplies back and forth.
They are most generous with their time and energy.
The staff is full of praise and glad to be here making their
contribution.
I am so honored to have my small part of this worthwhile effort.

We were treated with a poem written by a mother, Anna.
There was pure music in her words and we were deeply moved.
Steve told "the Deer and the Raven" story with a lesson for us all.
I was happy to read my Dog Point history writings from my
collection.
Silently in the background the women prepared our wondrous meals.

Victor and friend brought in red snapper for our supper that night.
Red snapper nuggets with beach asparagus and rice cooked to
perfection.
Earlier we ate venison stew with a native plant salad enjoyed by
everyone.
The work continued on the drying sockeye which was cut in even
thinner
Pieces to aid in the drying and I was given samples from time to time.

Playtime included kayak paddling in the bay and frisbee on shore.
A Littlefield tradition, baseball was played on the flats.
Two teams were selected and competition was fierce for a while.
Soon the score was 7 to 7 and then I scored the final home run at 8.
We used the cork ball and had such fun running after that cork.

We had fun and shared deep thoughts about where we are going.
The journey of life has many twists and turns which we carefully
travel.
Dog Point Fish Camp helps us get a perspective on where we want to
go.
We hope we give the children hope to go forward with their lives.
They are the beauty we see as the process of growing up.

THE DAY AT DOG POINT

Excitement runs wild with the flow of Dog Point.
Minds intent on teaching are tuned to a fine pitch.
A rain--soaked trip up the bay for deer took place.
Right around the bend we saw what appeared to be a buck.
Dog salmon moving toward the river jumped to look where they are.

The 223 Rifle is sighted in and ready for work.
Careful loads of ammunition are at the ready for deer
The gray countryside is a gathering mist before our eyes.
Shearwater birds are fishing for small fish and diving.
Ryan is hopeful of getting in some Tlingit hunting experience.
His young eyes look intently between rain drops and hopeful.

The seal rock is vacant as they are out fishing for salmon.
Unfortunately, other hunters are ahead of us scaring the game.
I use the gun case to keep my hands warm during our traveling.
Sharp raindrops at great boat speed slap our faces.
We squint ahead looking for a chance to find game.
Passing the mouth of Nakawsina sound we head up the straits.

Diane, Joy and Martina are here for the weekend of adventure.
They acquaint themselves with each other, telling their life stories.
They add much interest to the camp with rich experiences.
Ryan listens intently gathering life experiences from them.
He is our main man to share our lives with for this camp.

Ryan really enjoyed sighting in the 223 rifle.
He said it was the highlight of his trip to camp.
It is no secret because his instructor made it easy for him.
Careful preliminary setting up to shoot were very important.
Starting out prepared was all the difference in the world.

Franklin James is here and an active contributor to the camp.
He taught Tlingit gestures, adding a definite dimension to the study.
The camp joined in his seminar of thrilling Tlingit lifestyle.
We consider ourselves indeed blessed by exposure to him.
He had a rich humor and wisdom we all cherish.
As for myself I get so much extra out of being here.
Just around the corner, my favorite bay where I first fish camped.
Ralph and Elsie Young took me there in my eighth and ninth year.
The camp was my introduction to Tlingit food preparation.
Heads, tail, and backbone dinners was our reward.
It was like owning a country where people lived in harmony.
Community living of caring neighbors is what we knew.
Sharing what we caught in fish and game opened my little eyes.
I now carry this sense of sharing to this very day.
I have a heavy respect for my Elders as I should.

Dog Point Fish Camp some day will have graduates returning.
This is something I would like to see in my lifetime.
My own children enjoyed it so much along with their friends.
Decades of children came here to learn and share culture.
And it was completely open to all who cared to come.

The first morning we saw little brown creepers, black--backed
Chickadees, and the evening wren. Their food was blue berries.
Fishing kingfishers are always in the bay catching food.
When hunting they literally hover motionless above their prey.
Jumping humpies pass the Cove on their way to the river.

After serving years of service as a night watchman, Tank is gone.
The dog kept the camp free of bears and other predators.
Its wild streak was its undoing, namely biting others.
We feel a sadness at its leaving but understand why.
The dog had a keen interest in everything going on.

It was my pleasure to read some of my poetry for the camp.
It included my eulogy for my nephew "TJ".
The memorial poem for a Kaagwaantaan lady still affects me deeply.
Diane read some of her moving work she has had published.

THE DAILY DOG POINT

Daily we work as hard as we play at Dog Point.
There are fish to be split, filleted and hung.
Alder wood must have bark peeled.
Fires must be the right temperature
The smoke needs to be dense enough to work.

After lunch I gave my poetic efforts to the crowd.
They were most gracious toward my work.
It's the most important work I've ever done. After all,
It's the center of my Tlingit universe.
It's the best part of the last part of my life.

Today the Dog Point Dancers performed to a select crowd.
It was open house for the camp.
A grand lunch of seal meat, Athabaskan ice cream,
Herring egg salad, fried bread and rice was given.
The cooks basked in a warm stream of praise.

To the delight of camp our visitors took part in play time.
The Daunhauser's displayed their considerable kayak skills.
Tom and Phil from Angoon took to the water boats.
Andy Hope III skillfully skipped rocks and frisbeed.
Martin Strand did some significant wading.

During the visit Uncle Colby took out two young hunters.
They took the alpine trail north of town.
They saw one good deer but could not see the horns.
Claudette Brady left camp only to return looking radiant.
Della Charney, ANS President made miniature cedar hats.

Ted Wright, a great Sitkan, seemed at home here.
Visitors from Arizona and North Carolina rejoiced in the sun.
Patty from Juneau was here before and added to the fun.
A visitor from Japan showed an interest in caviar.
Camp projects continued throughout it all.

PULLING THE FUTURE OUT OF MY PAST
July, 2000

The love of my un-lived life blossoms when I reach Dog Point.
A strong magnet of longing lingers inside me to be there.
It is beautiful reality and fantasy that leads me to this place.
Living close to Nature is all I ask of my remaining life.
The magic of my youthful days lives in powerful ways now.

Ancient Tribal yearnings build in my mind as I think of grandparents.
Oh the lessons learned by watching and listening as a young you.
Patient grandparents pulled me past childhood distractions.
It was hard but I was rewarded for paying attention.
DSI found out why we catch fish and hunt for game in time.

I was given responsibilities the same as others in the camp.
Now as a grandparent I pass on the lessons with sensitivity and care.
Back then we were assigned duties and did them without question.
We believed our Elders and held them in high regard.
Their years spoke volumes of deep experience living off the land.

This is Dog Point Fish Camp, the gift of Roby and John Littlefield.
They give to the community and beyond this cultural experience.
Years and months of preparation they bring to the table.
In their complex lives they still have time to give more to us.
I hope they know they are appreciated by so many with our thanks.

Our commitment to succeed is what drives us to do our best.
Before I grew up to be a man I had my Nature vision.
I saw the good of a day's work while living off the land.
Our food preparation was to bring us to the future.
The positive attitudes of the Elders stay with us and are strong.

Caring minds planned the day.
Skilled hands put breakfast together
We talked of the work to come.
The fish and fame were in readiness.
Our lives are a work in progress.

In my mind I paint a picture of what we are doing.
It is a huge canvas with bold strokes of the brush.
Lighting our lives in a most colorful way.
In the shadows spirits of our Ancient ones smile upon us.
How can there be so much beauty in what we do?

CONCLUSION

As you have read carefully through all the articles that Martin wrote you might have noticed the theme, sometimes so subtly hidden, of a desire to really make a difference. He raises the question about the ultimate value to his life, and of his life to his many and varied occupations or interests. He saw in his grandfather, Ralph Young not only a deep cultural awareness but also a religious purpose where God and his relation to God is ultimately of importance. Martin saw this in his grandparents and likewise sees it in himself. Faith makes a difference.

As Martin has reached back through his generations to find meaning there is the almost quiet desire to have made a difference. It is as though he has been walking through the darkness with many lights shining and just to the side he sees his shadow, occasionally on one side and then on the other, sometimes walking behind him, sometimes with him and often in front of him, but always tied to himself through his feet.

His ability to see into and through a personality to the depth of meaning, the central purpose for life for each individual and for himself was one of the outstanding things about Martin. It is this editor's hope that the reader will be able to sit back and "muse" your own way through your life so far. As Martin sought an ultimate purpose, to what purpose has the reader put his or her life? You can even sit back in the midst of beautiful music, as did Martin and let the music guide you.

Martin's purpose in life will have been achieved if the reader assimilates or develops Martin's sense of concern for other individuals, regardless of their culture, status or position, and sees them as unique persons.

Ed